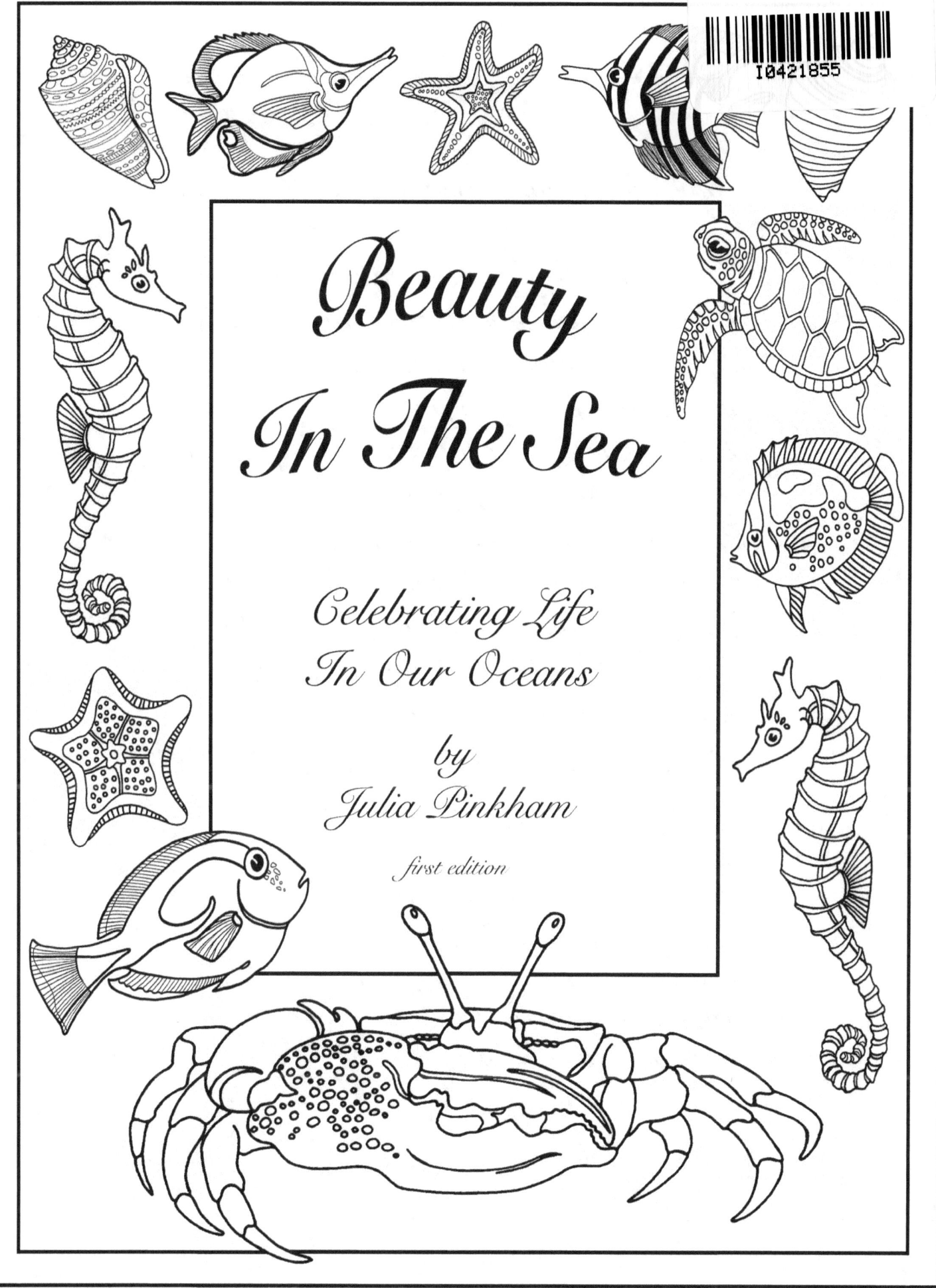

Beauty In The Sea

Celebrating Life In Our Oceans

by

Julia Pinkham

first edition

Coloring tips for "Beauty In The Sea":

Pages are blank on the back so color
 bleed-through won't affect the next image.
If you are coloring with marker pens
or like to use a lot of pressure,
place a blotter sheet between the pages
to protect them as you work.
In very small areas it is okay to fill
the entire shape with your colors. Try
putting in your highlights first.
Feel free to color with any colors you
desire, there are no rules!

Use blank pages at the end of the book to
experiment with your colors.

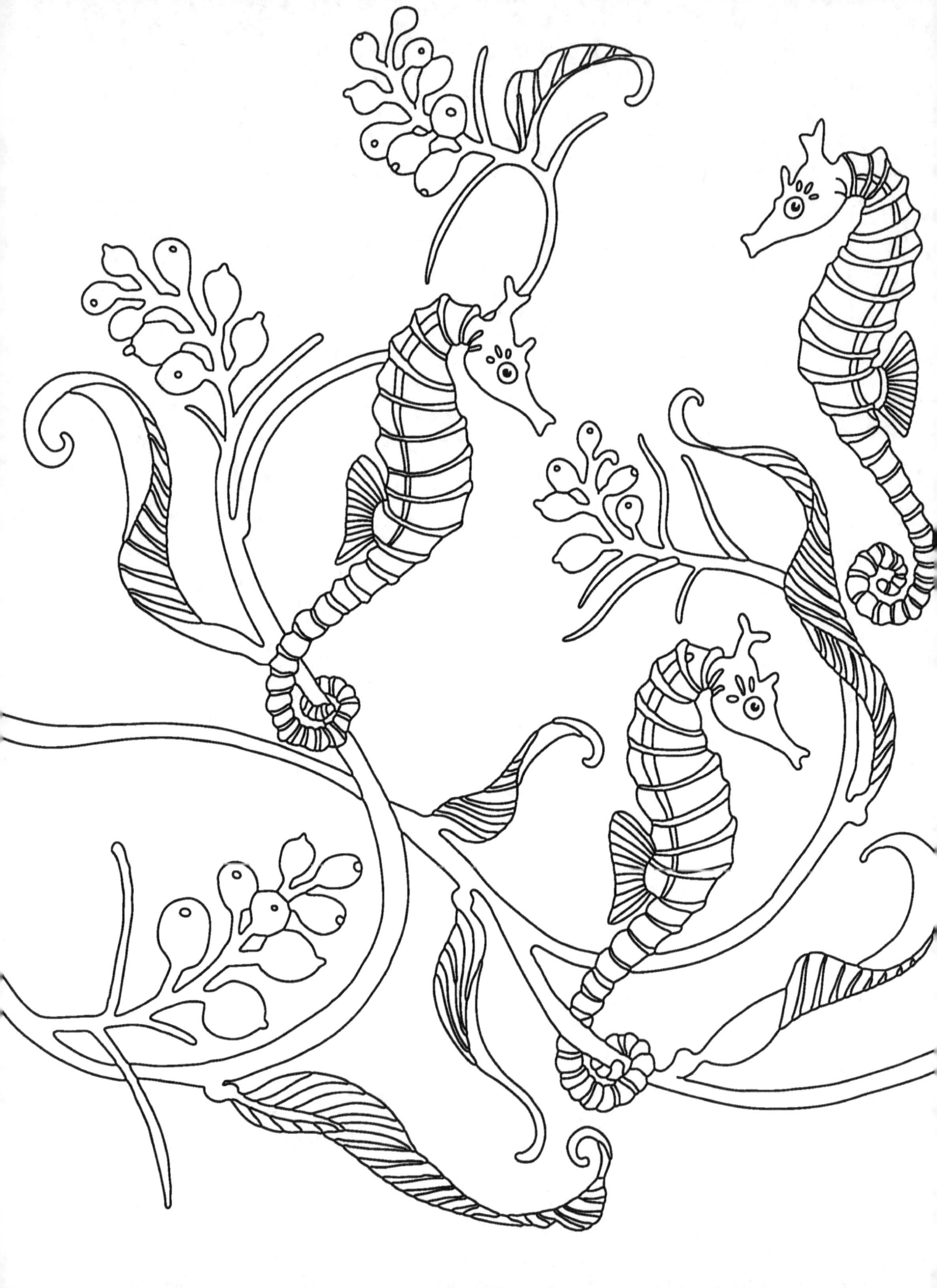

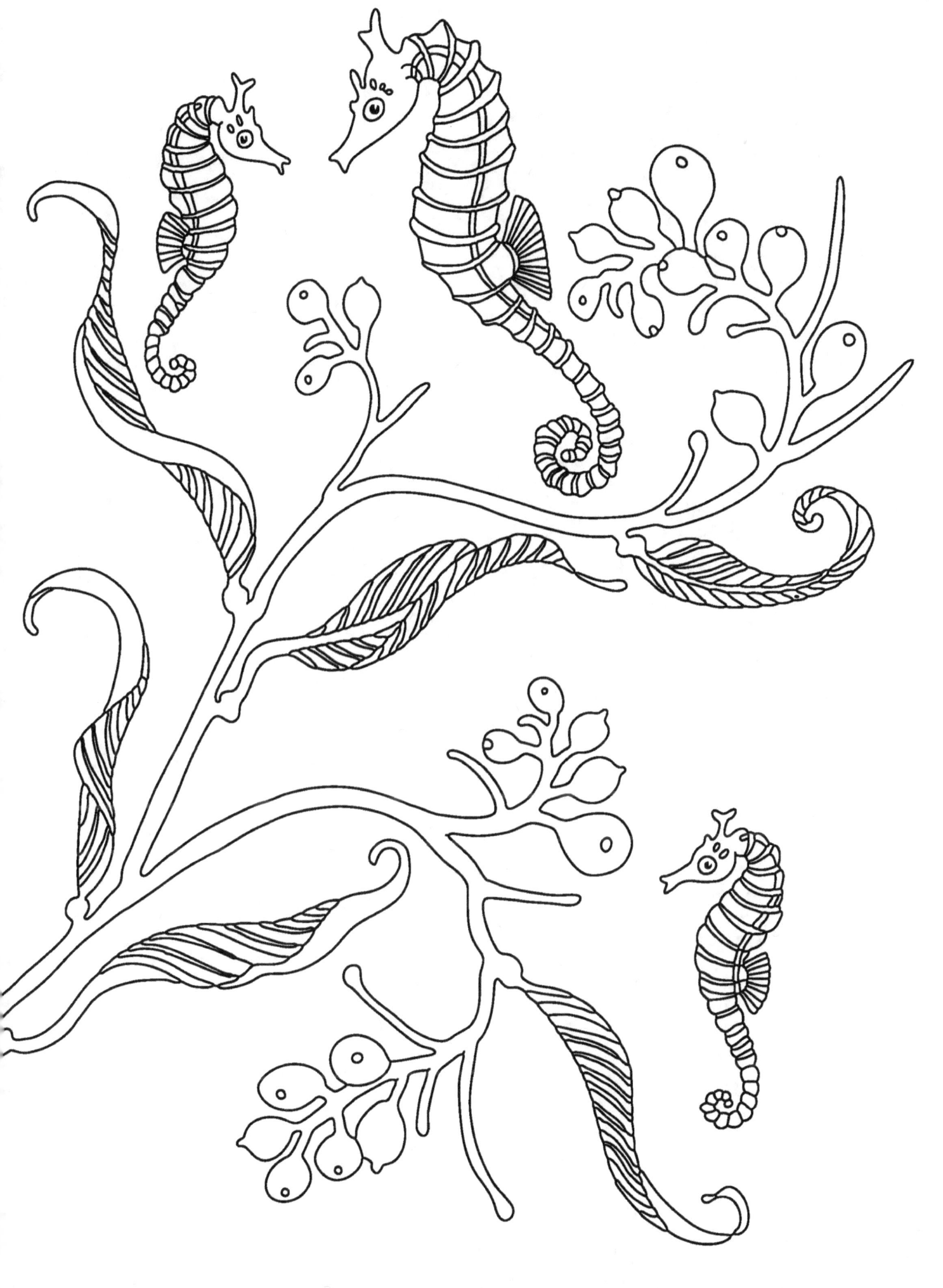

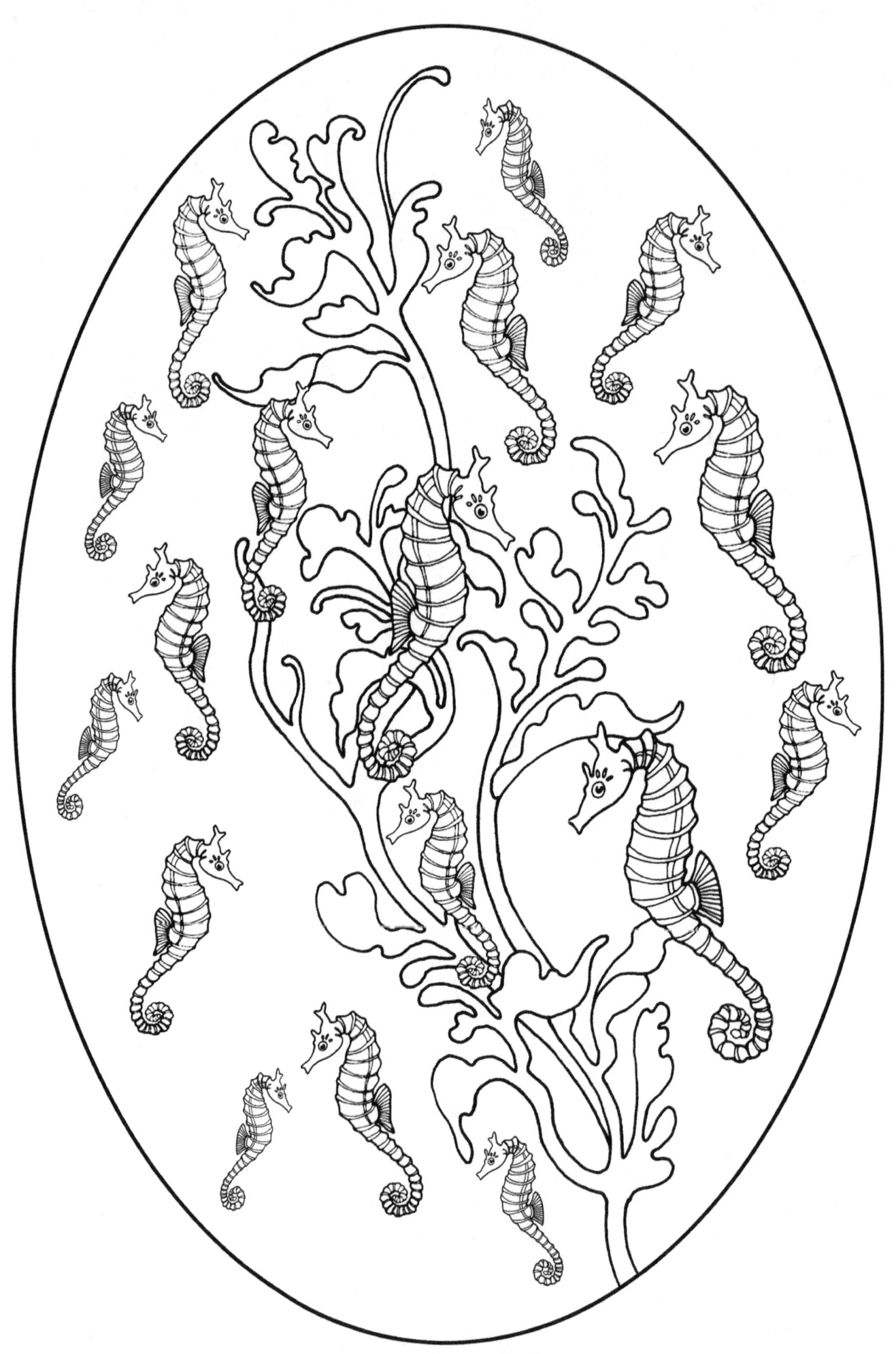

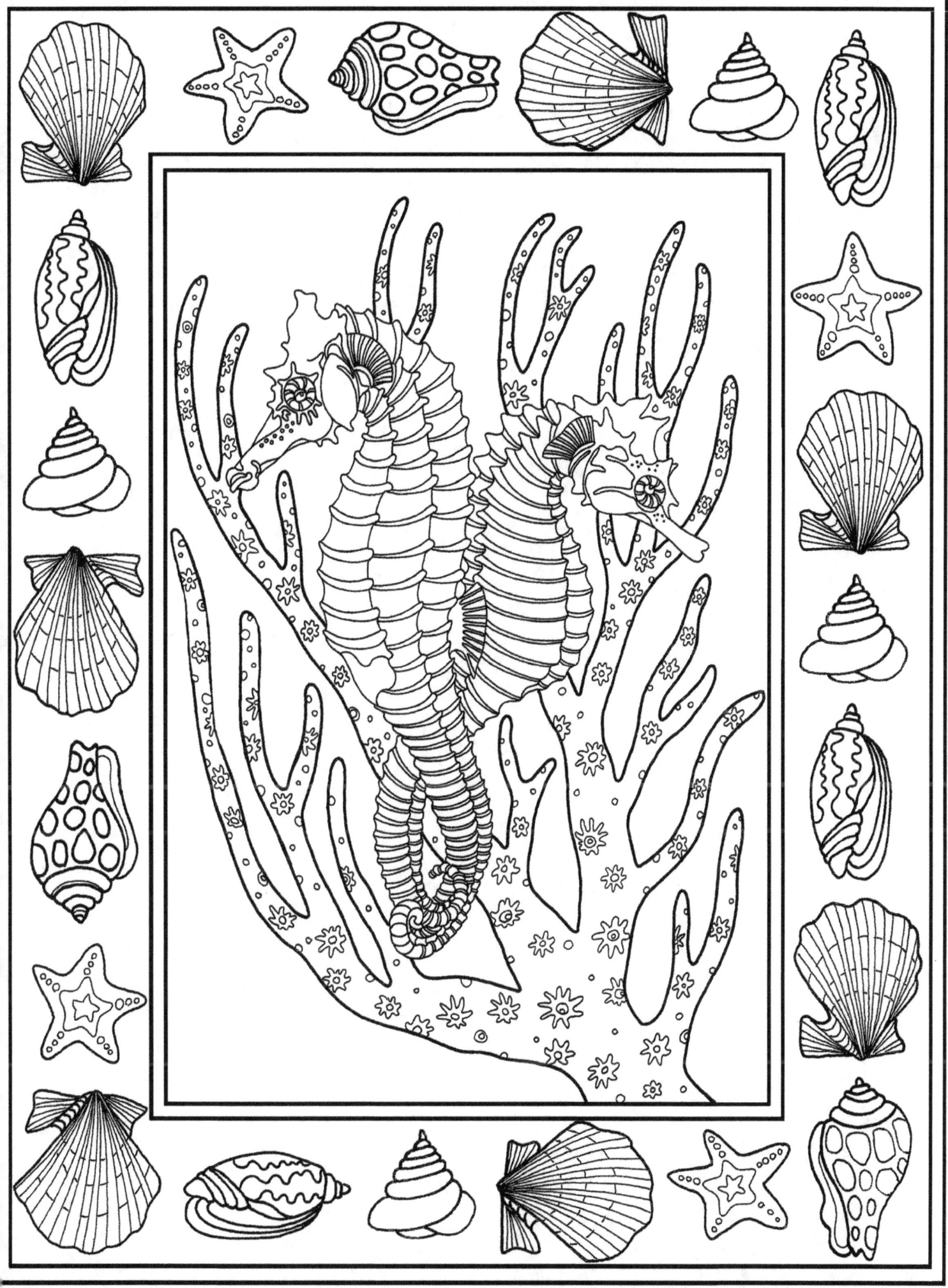

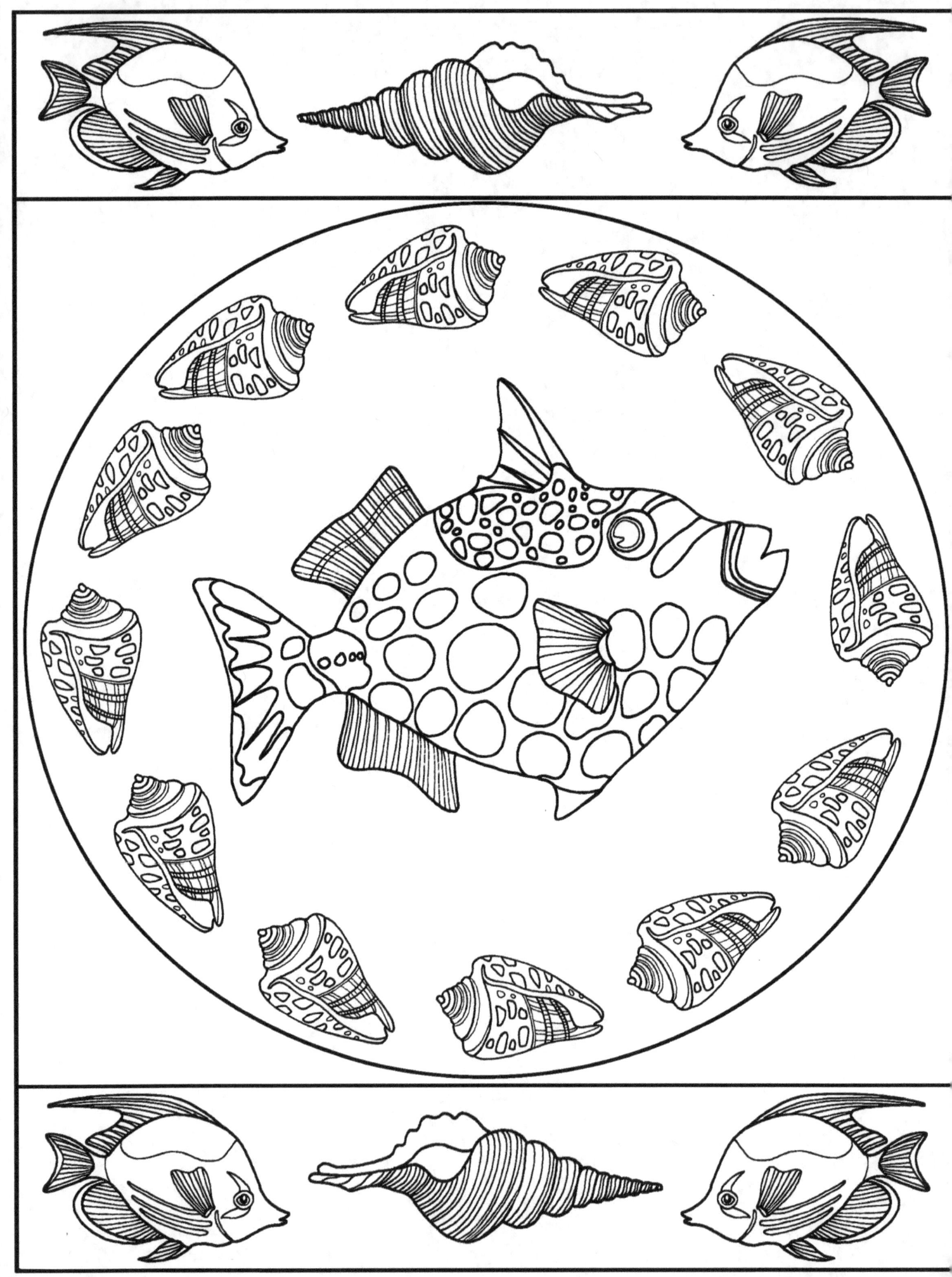

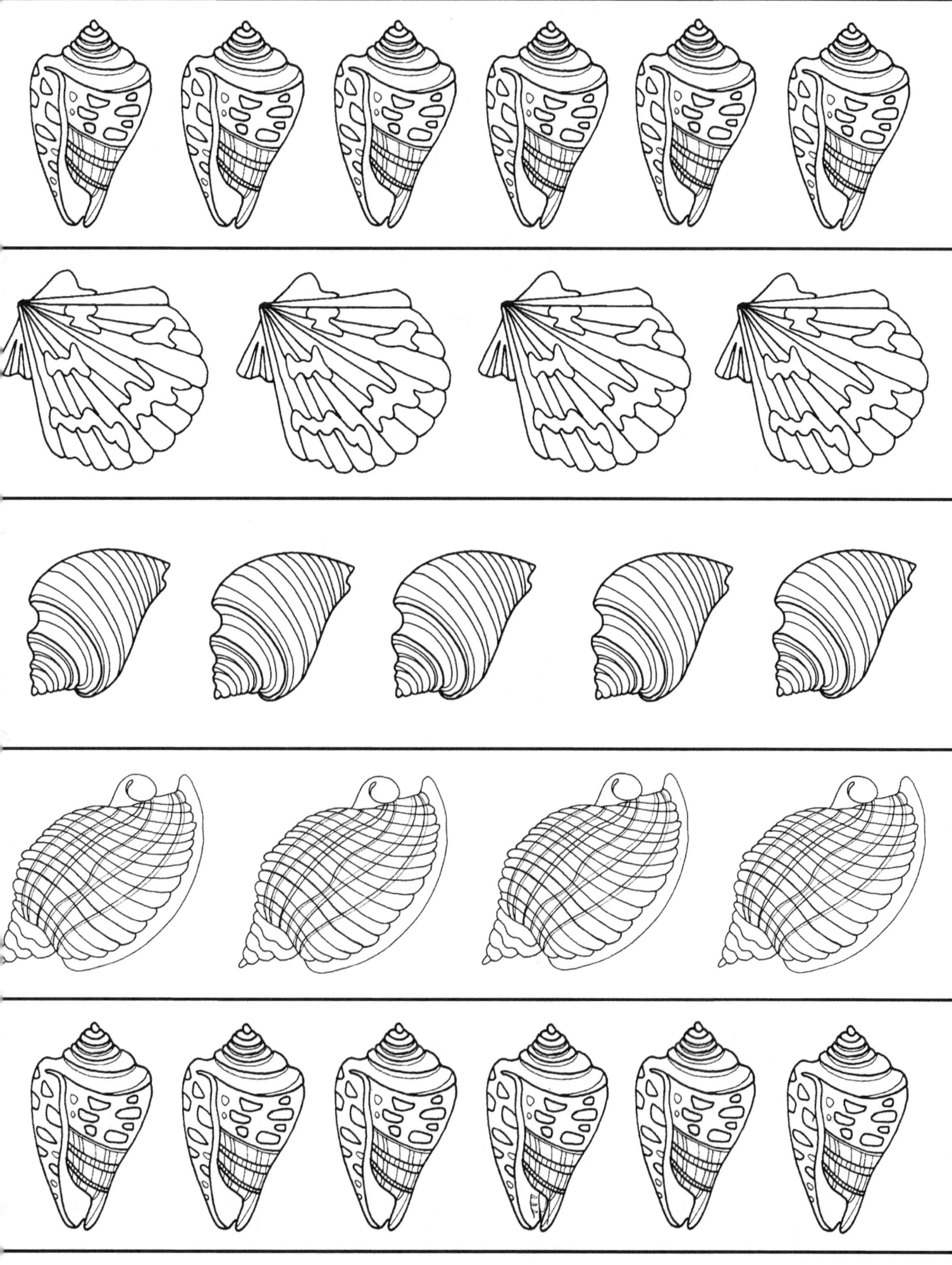

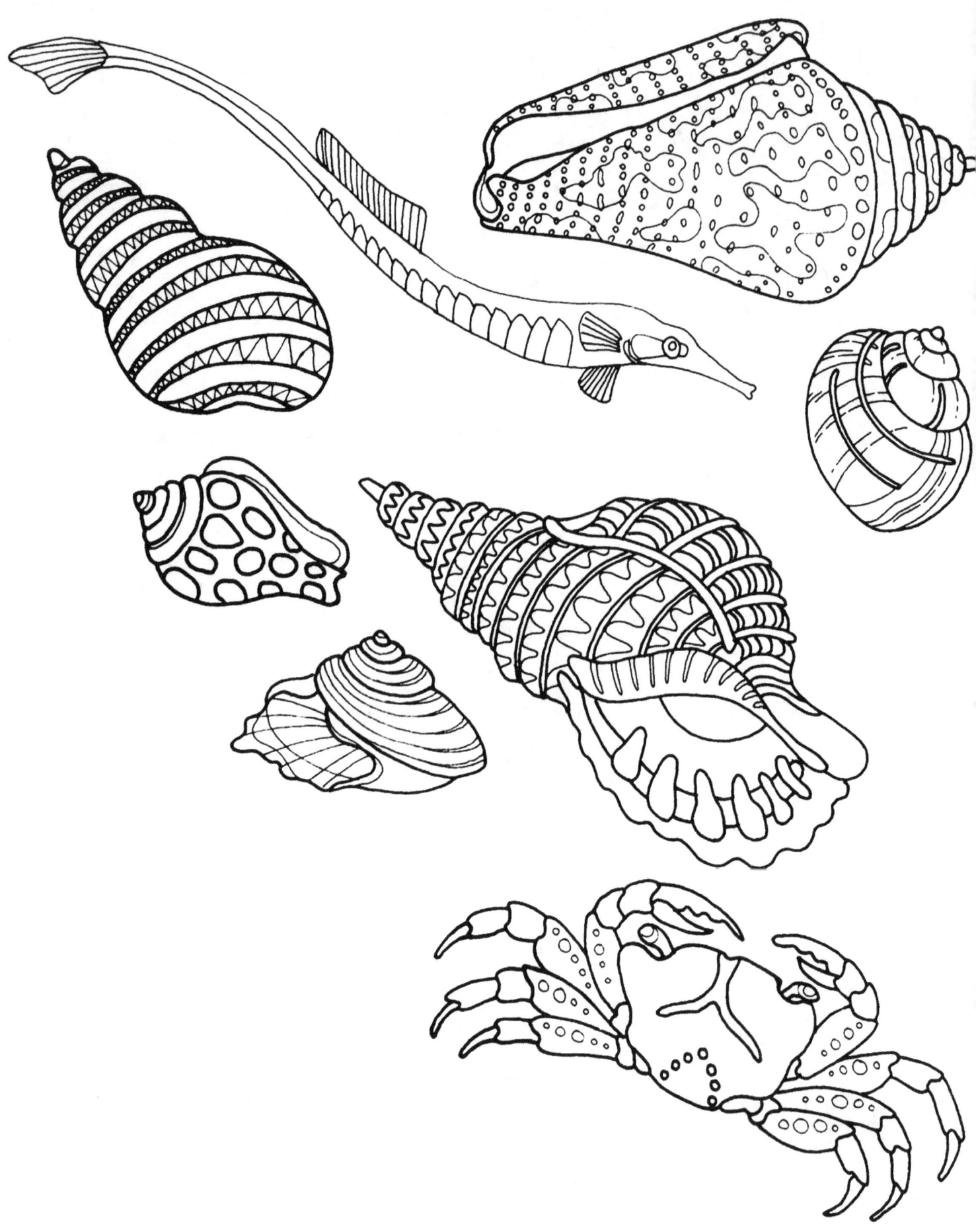

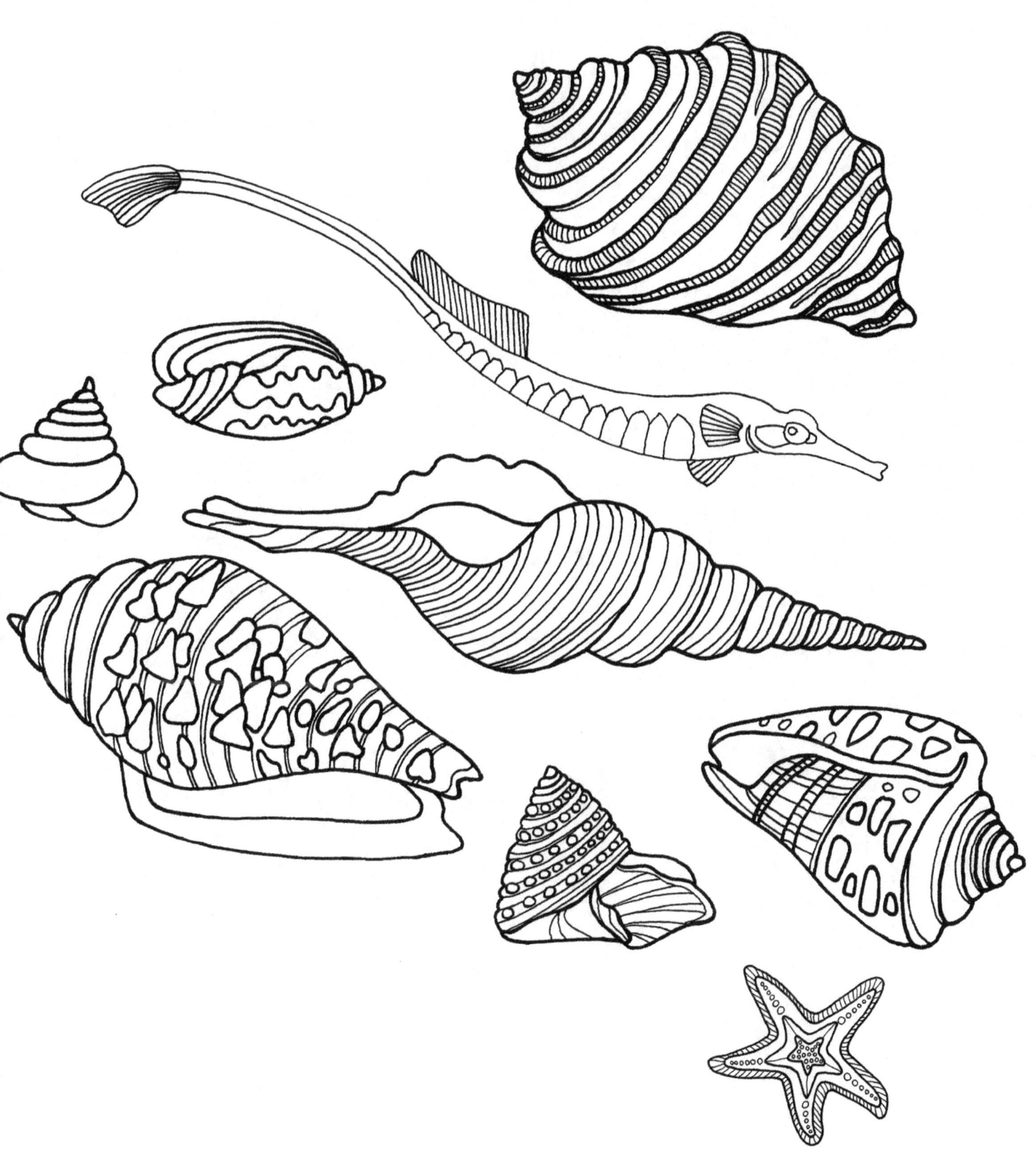

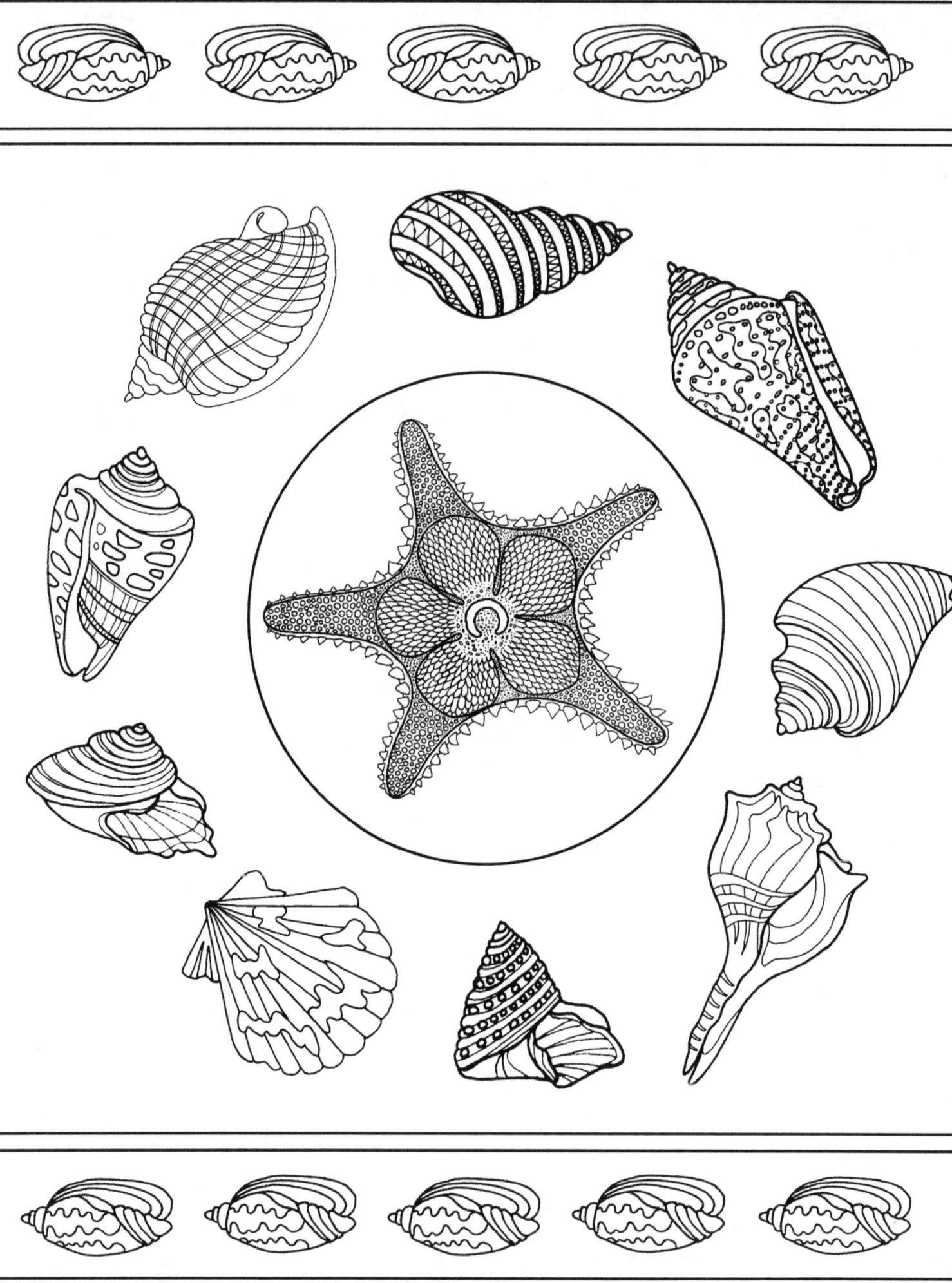

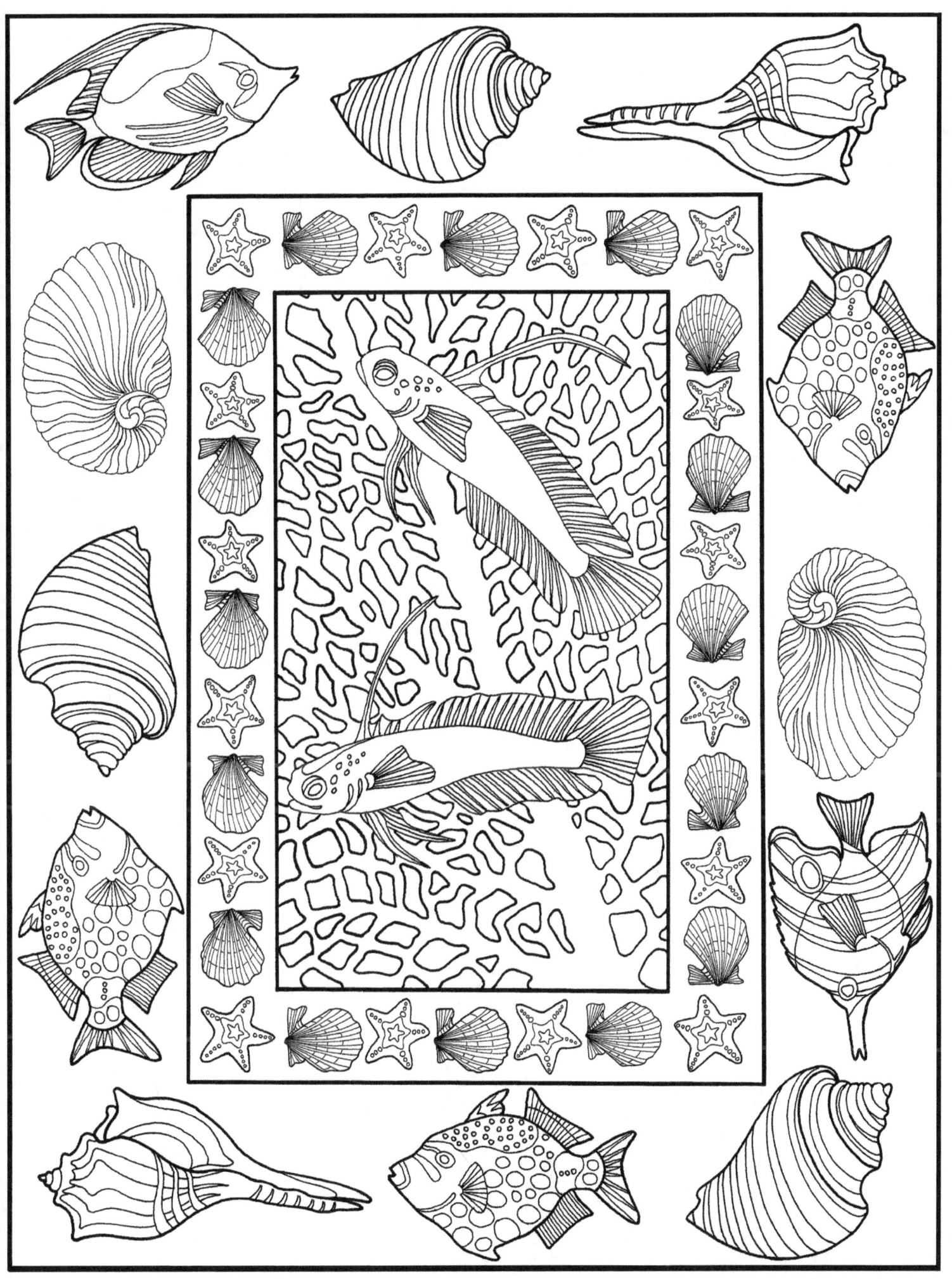

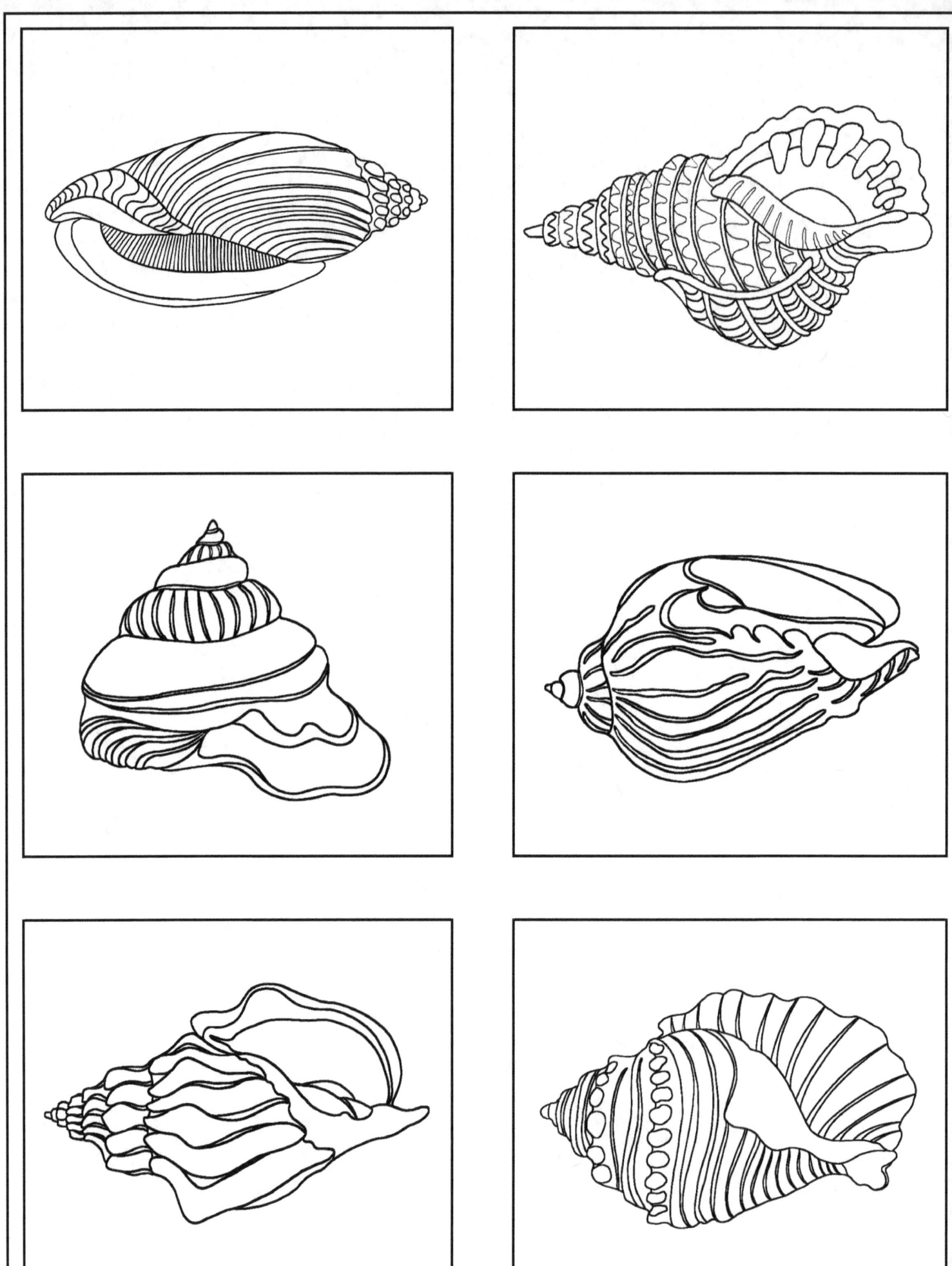

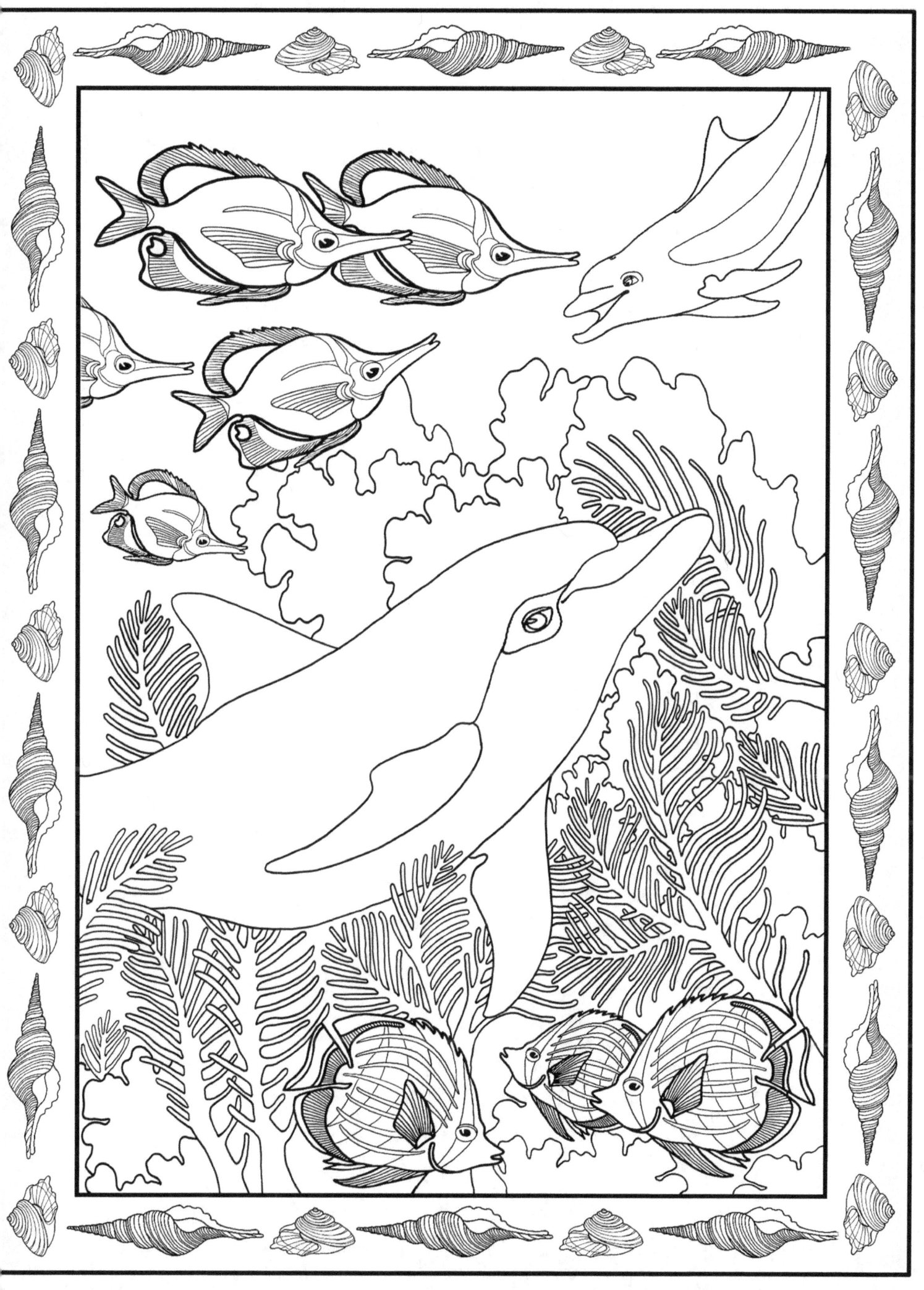

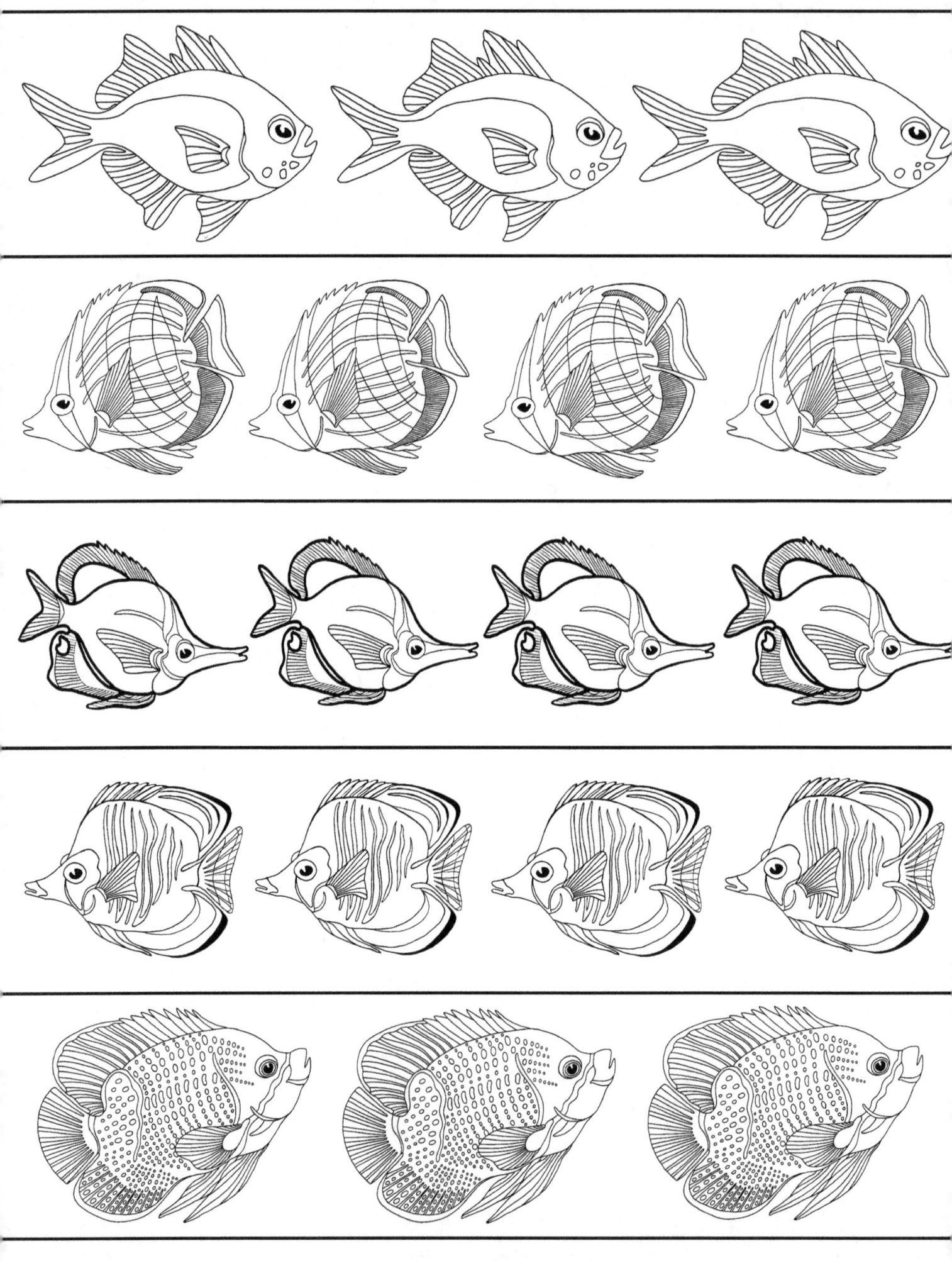

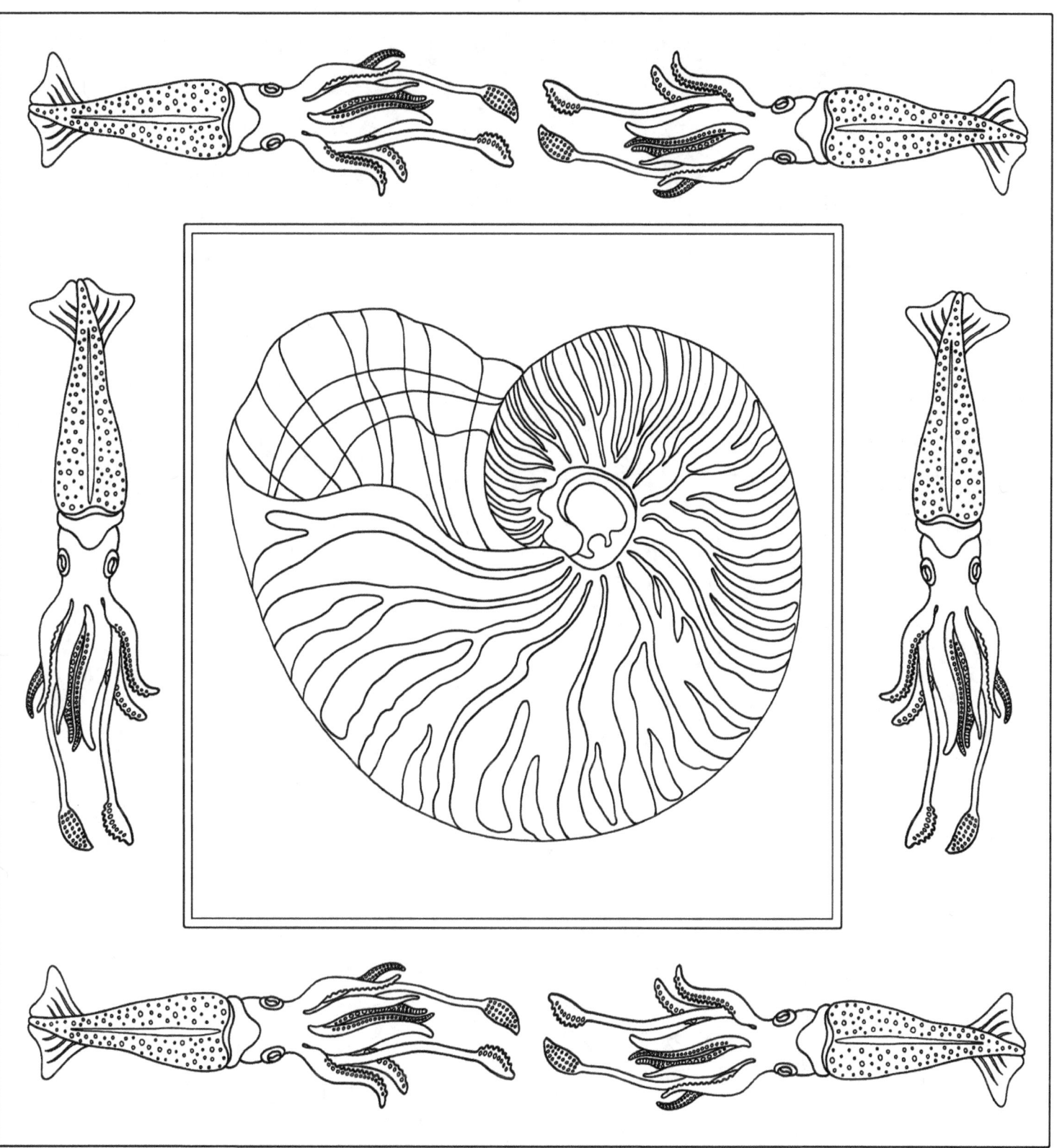

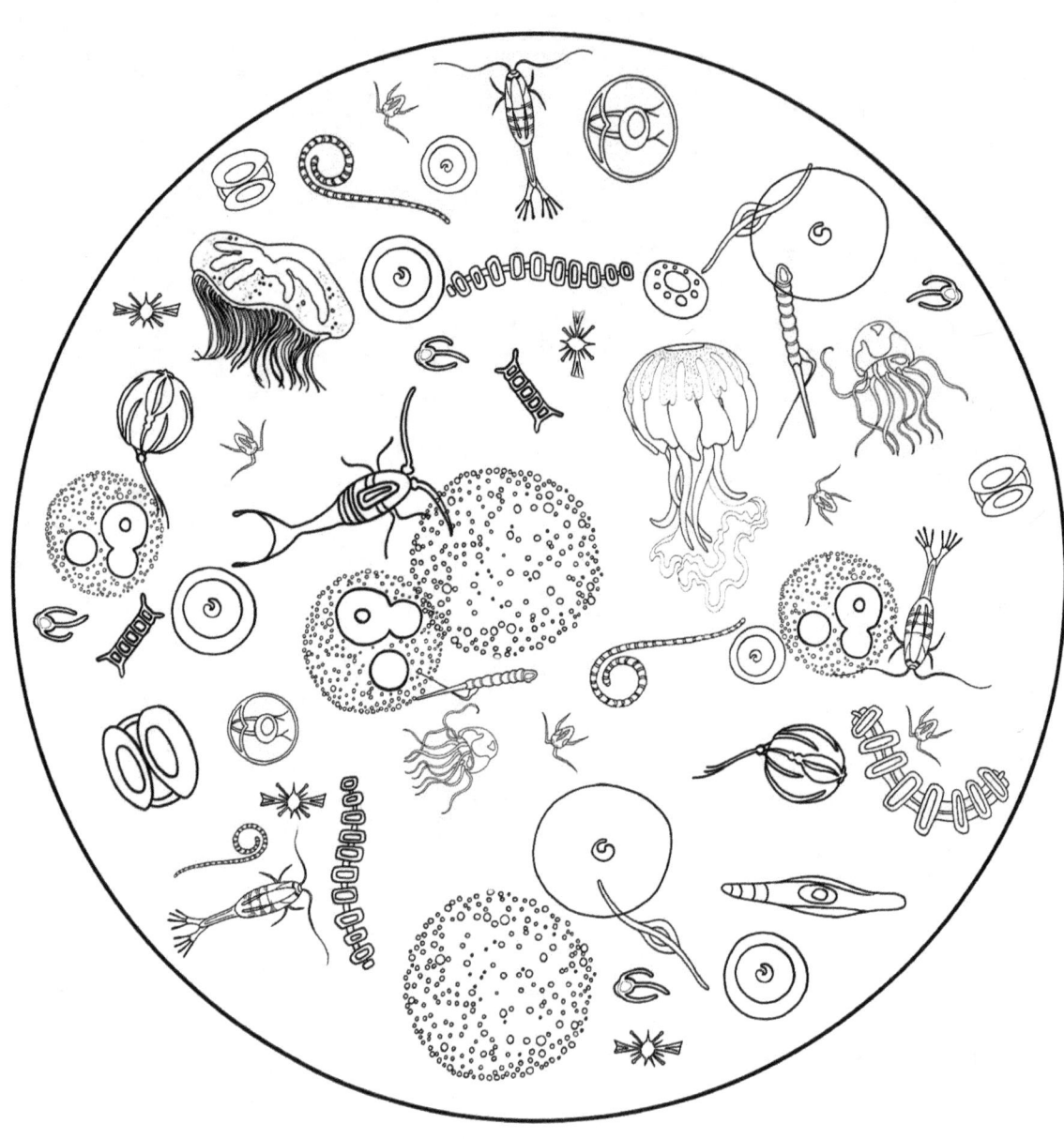

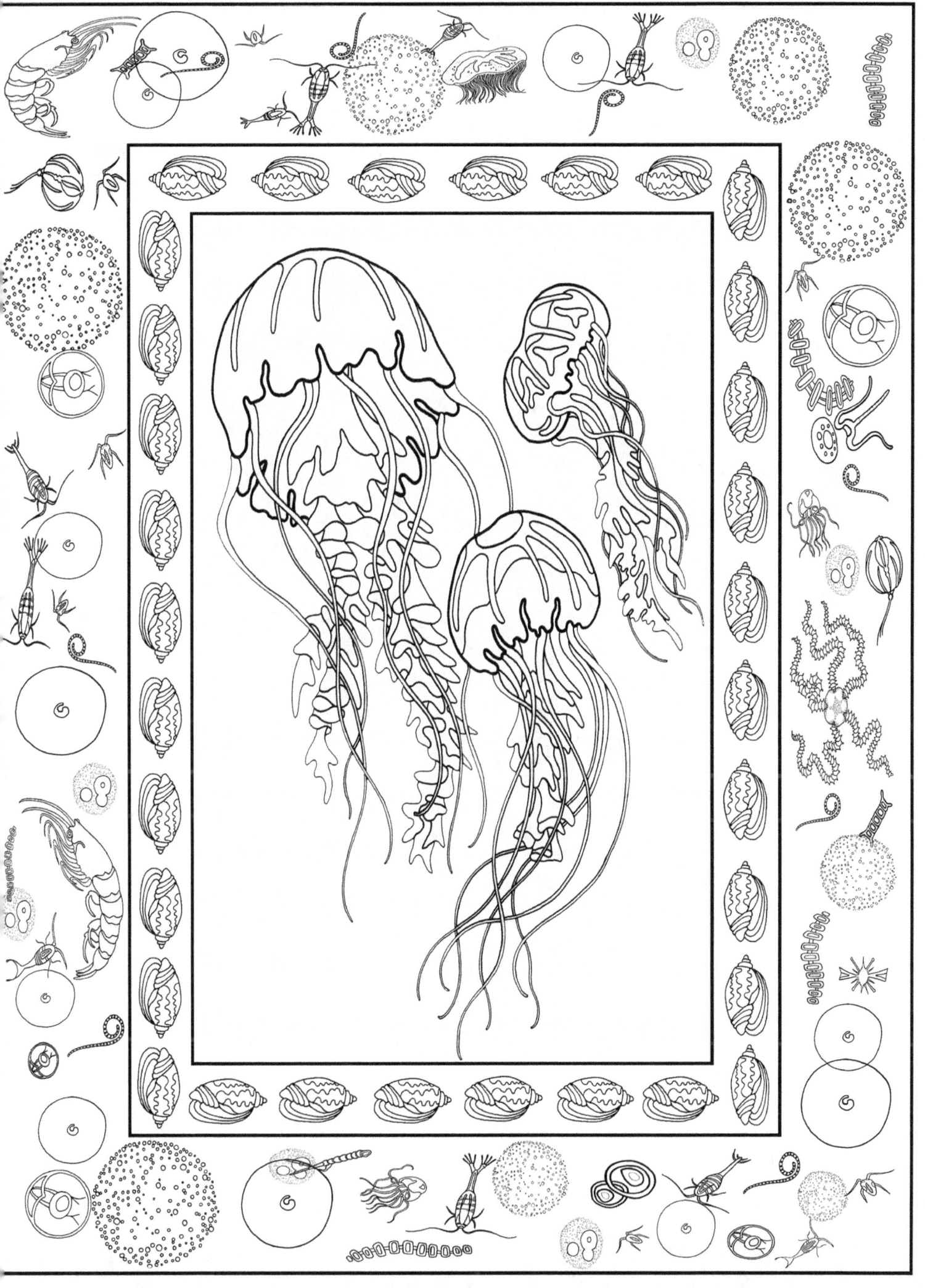

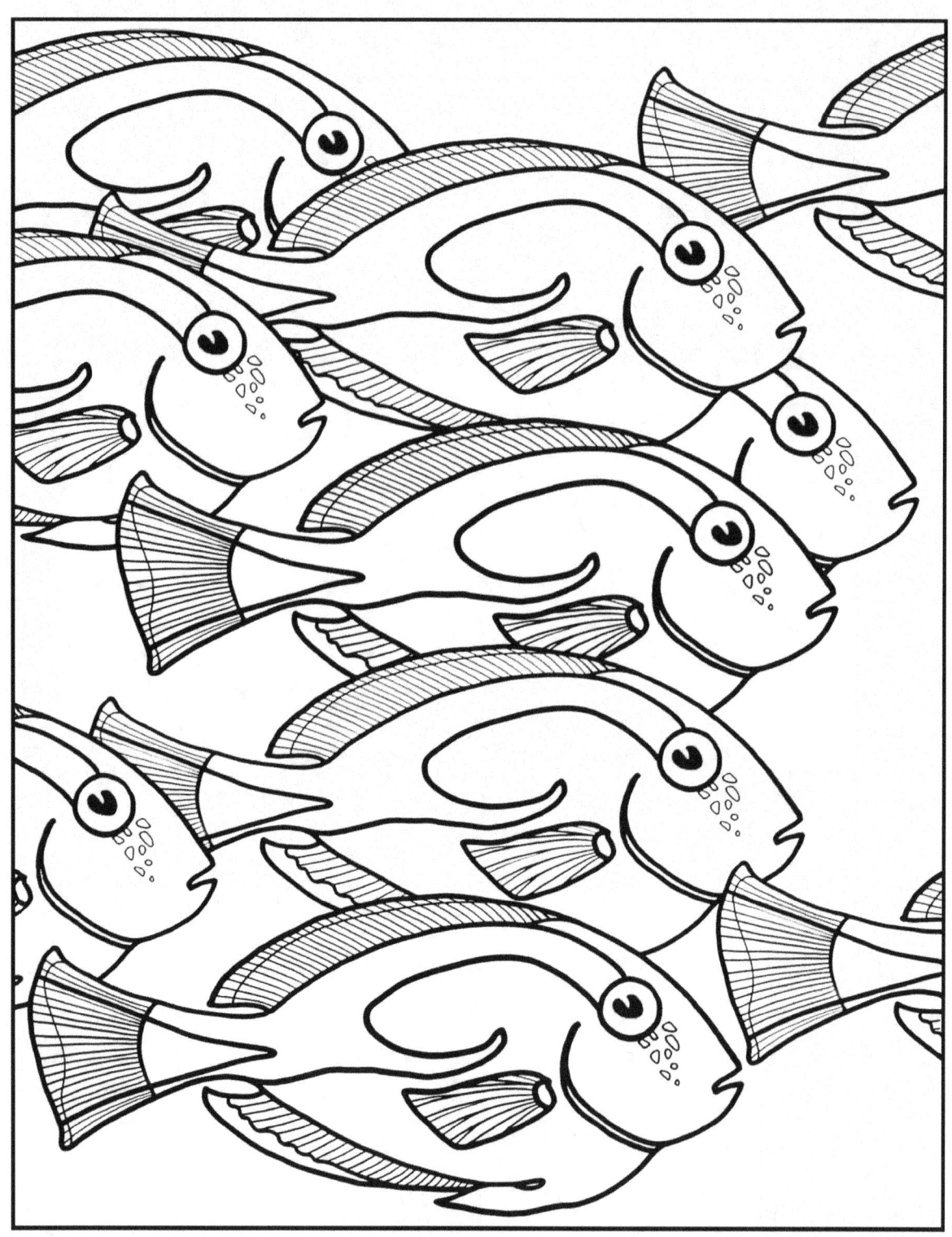

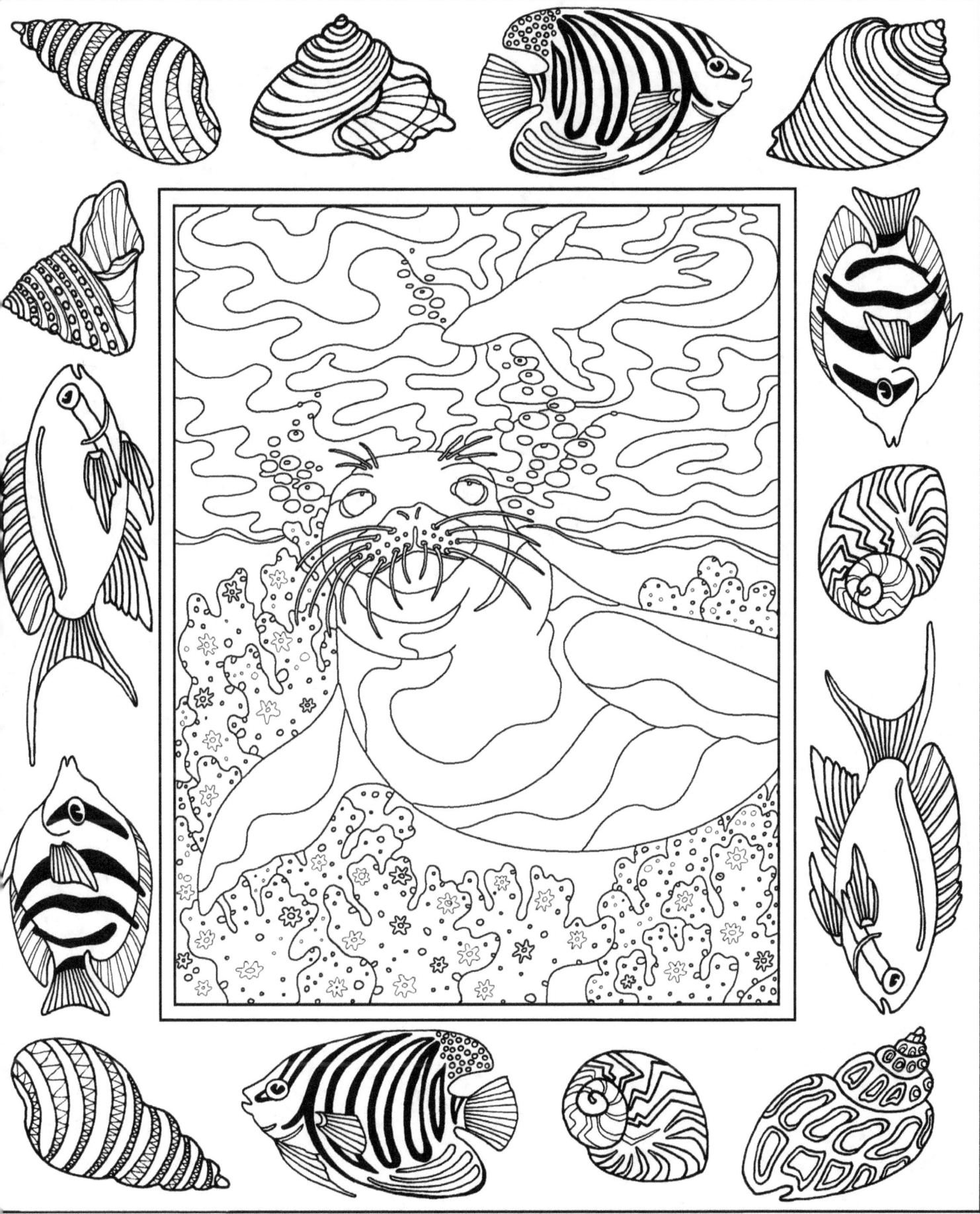

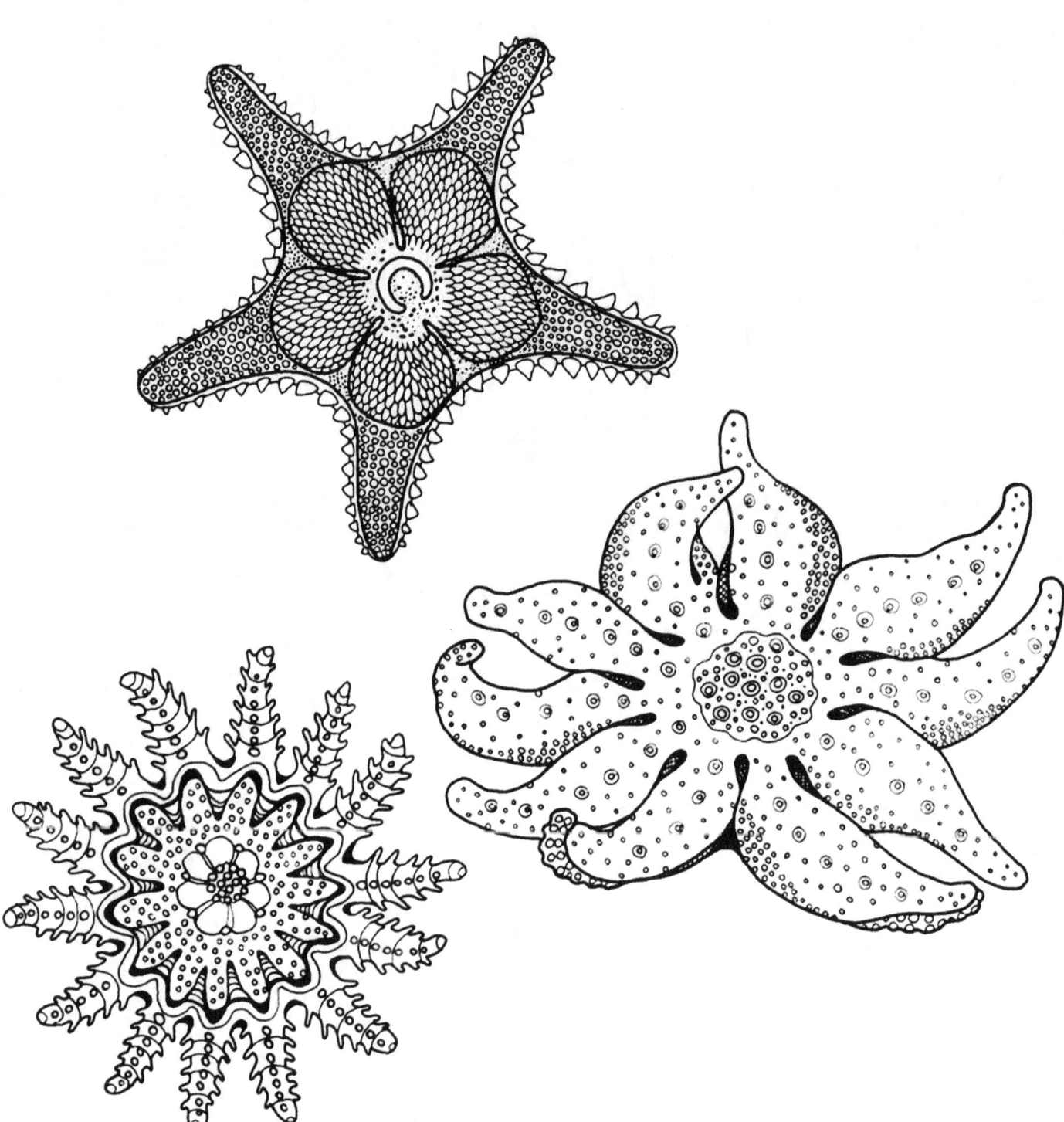

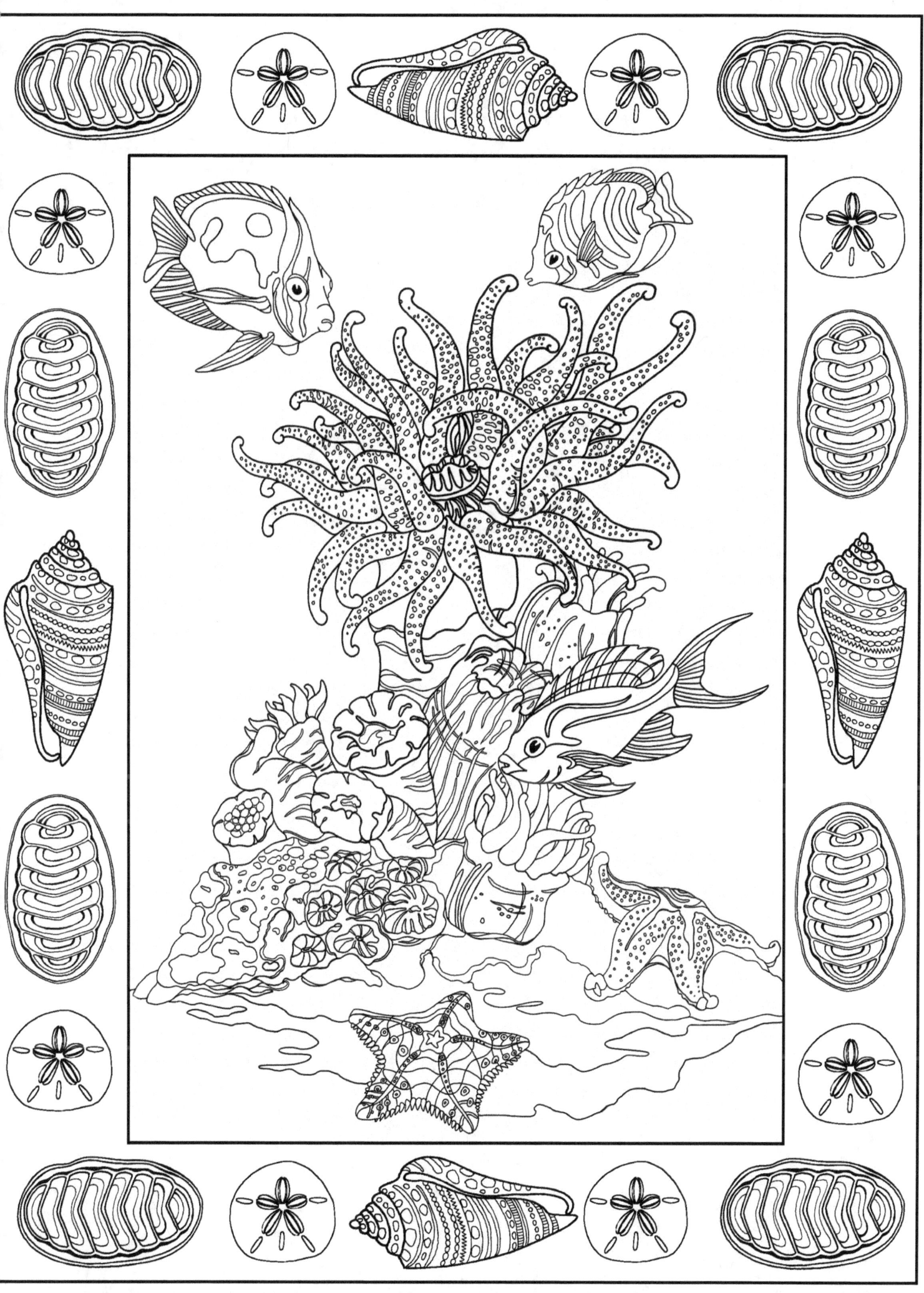

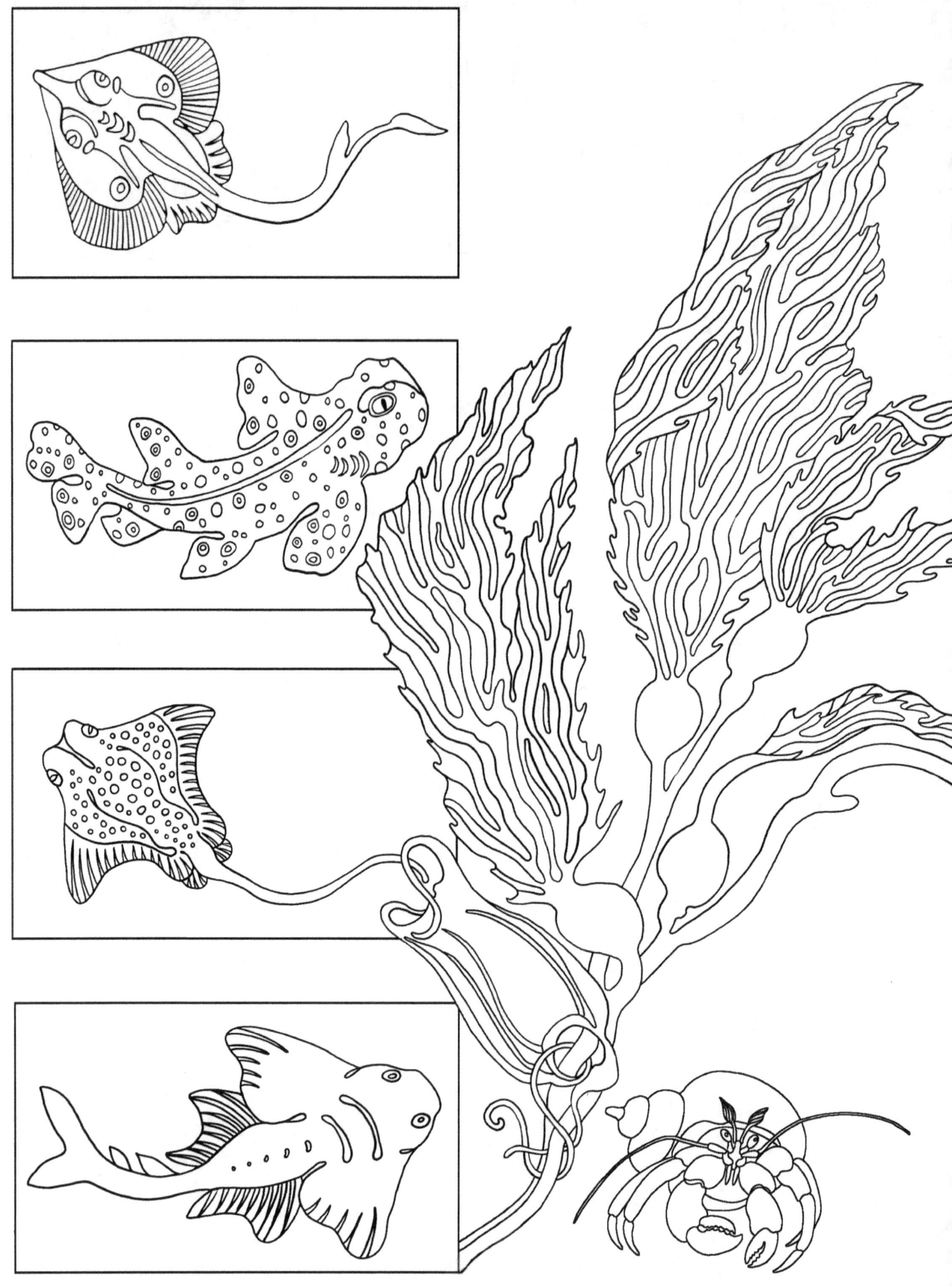

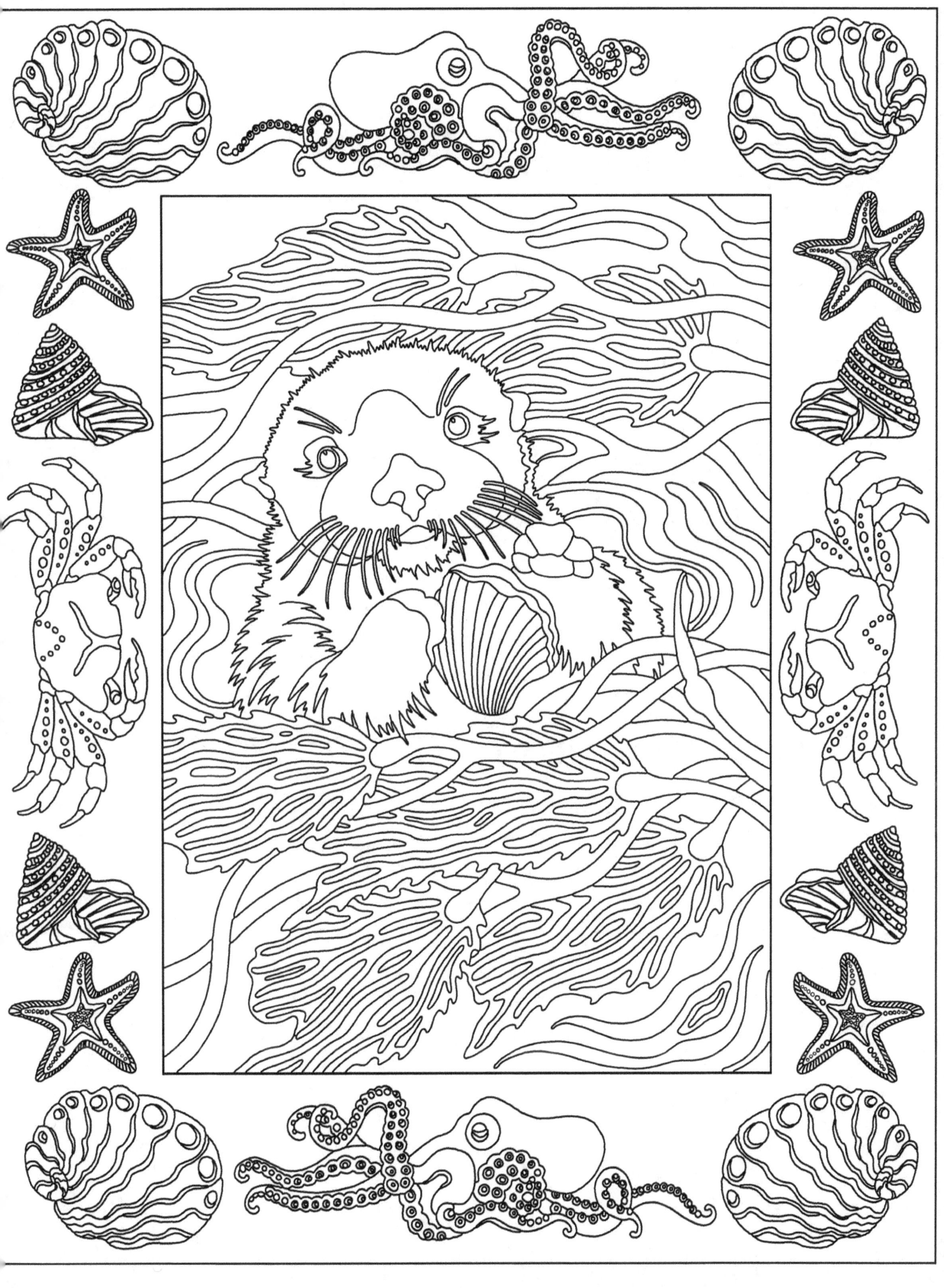

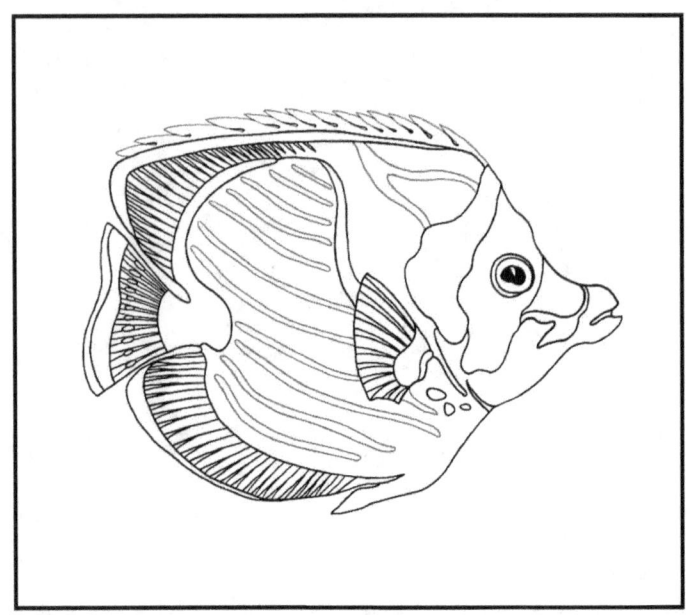
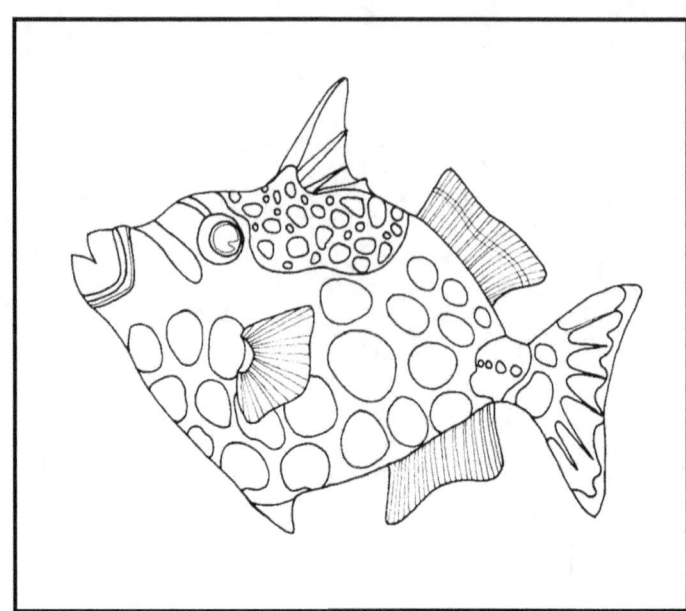
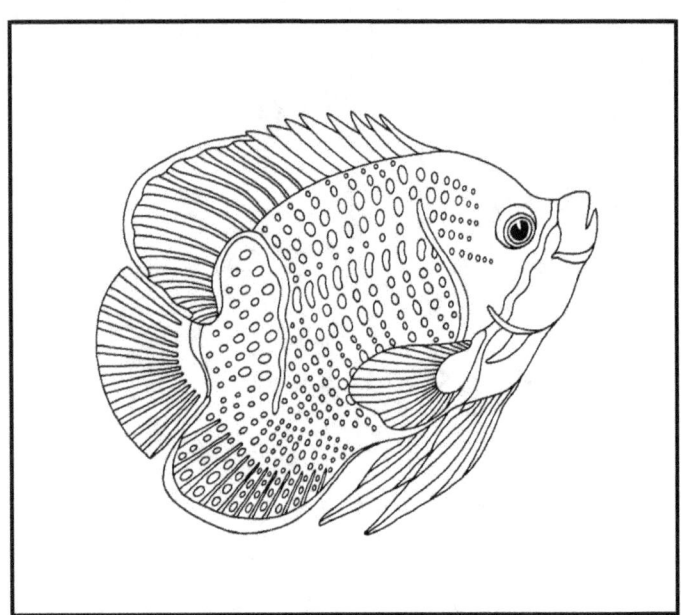
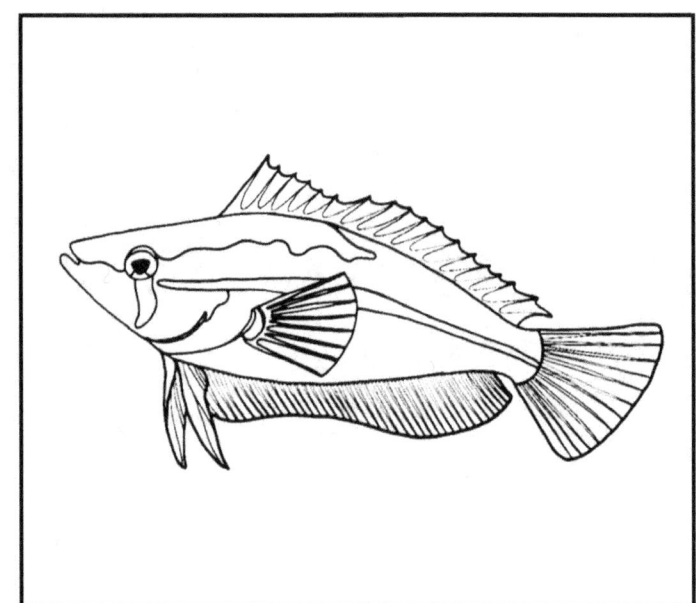
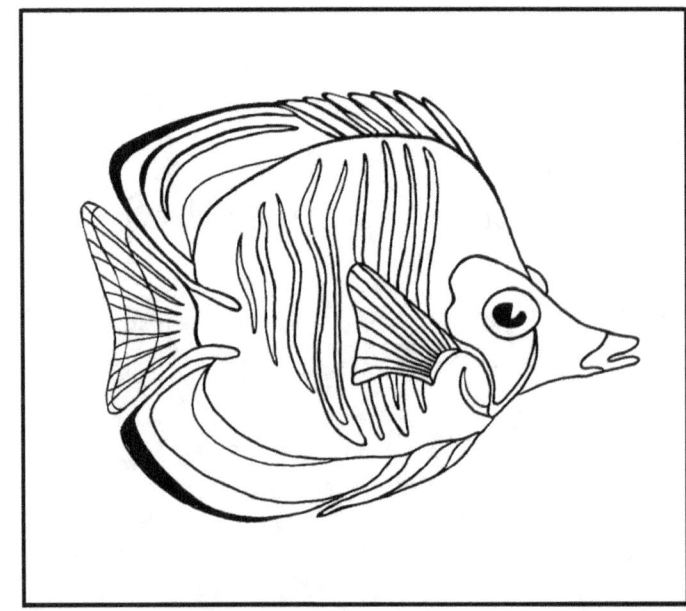
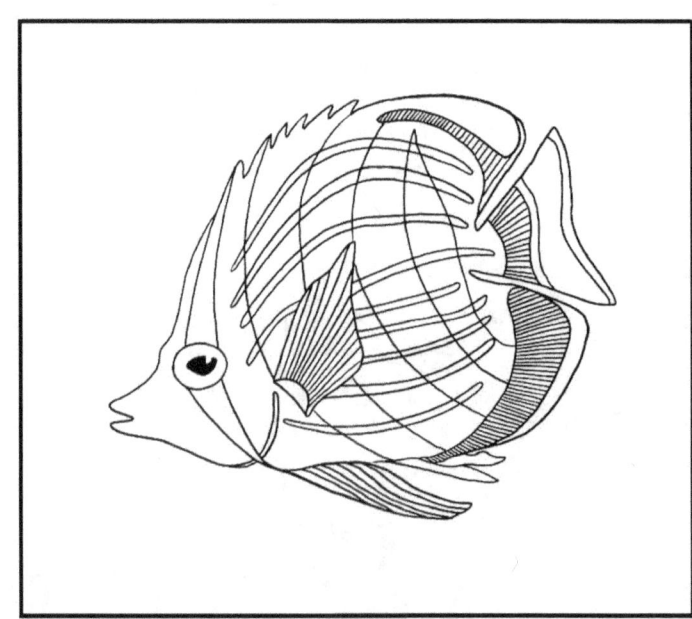

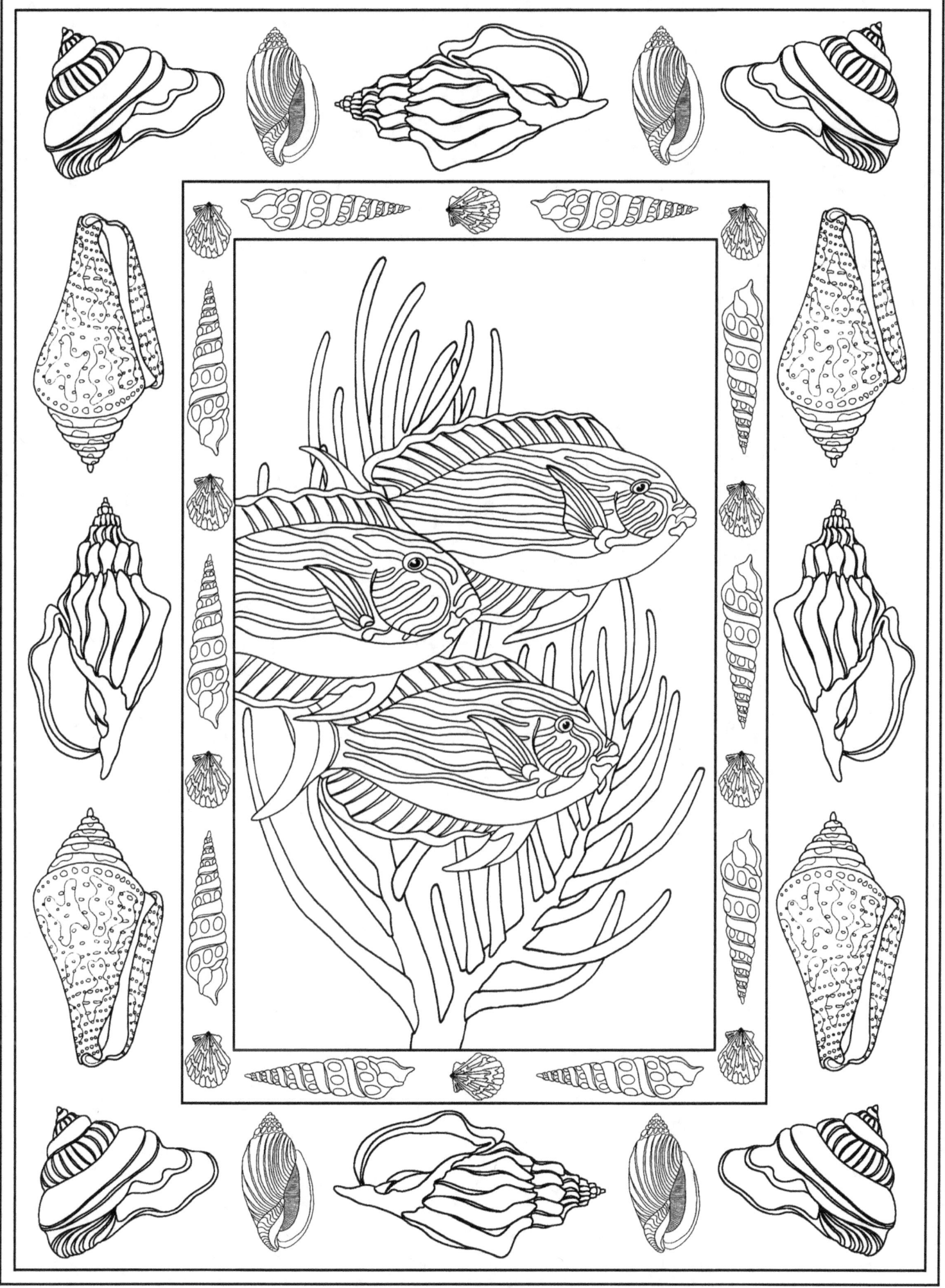

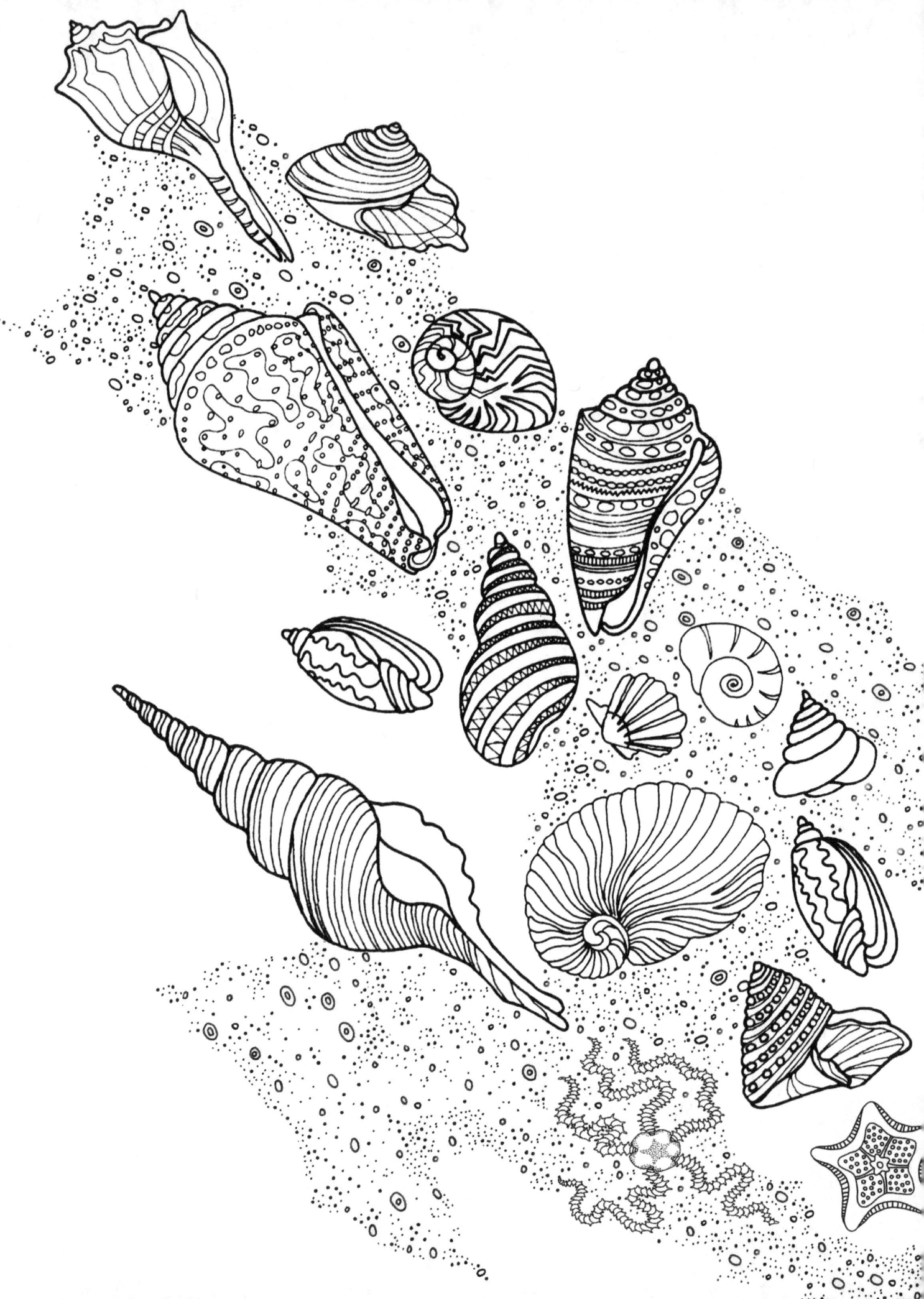

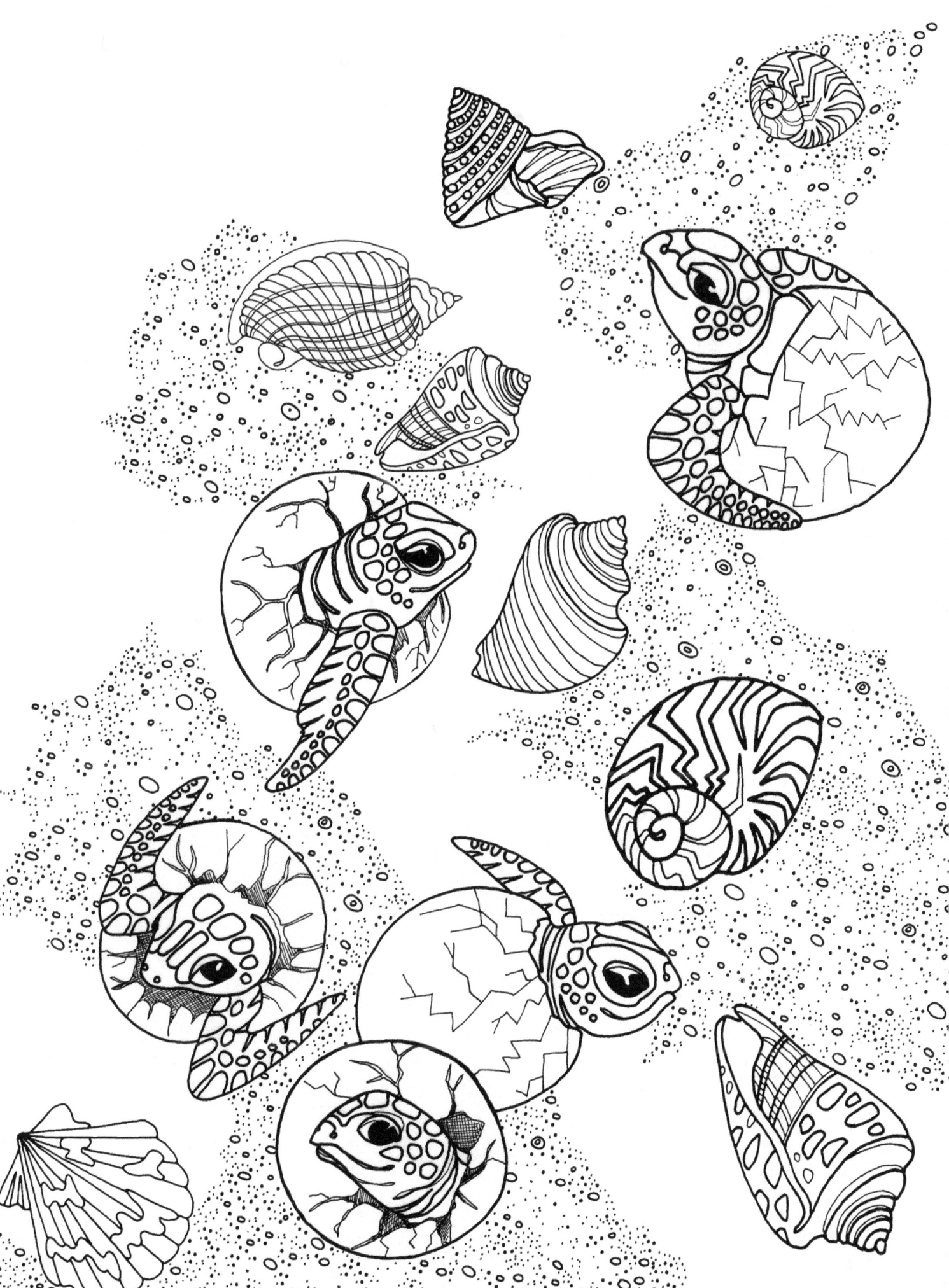

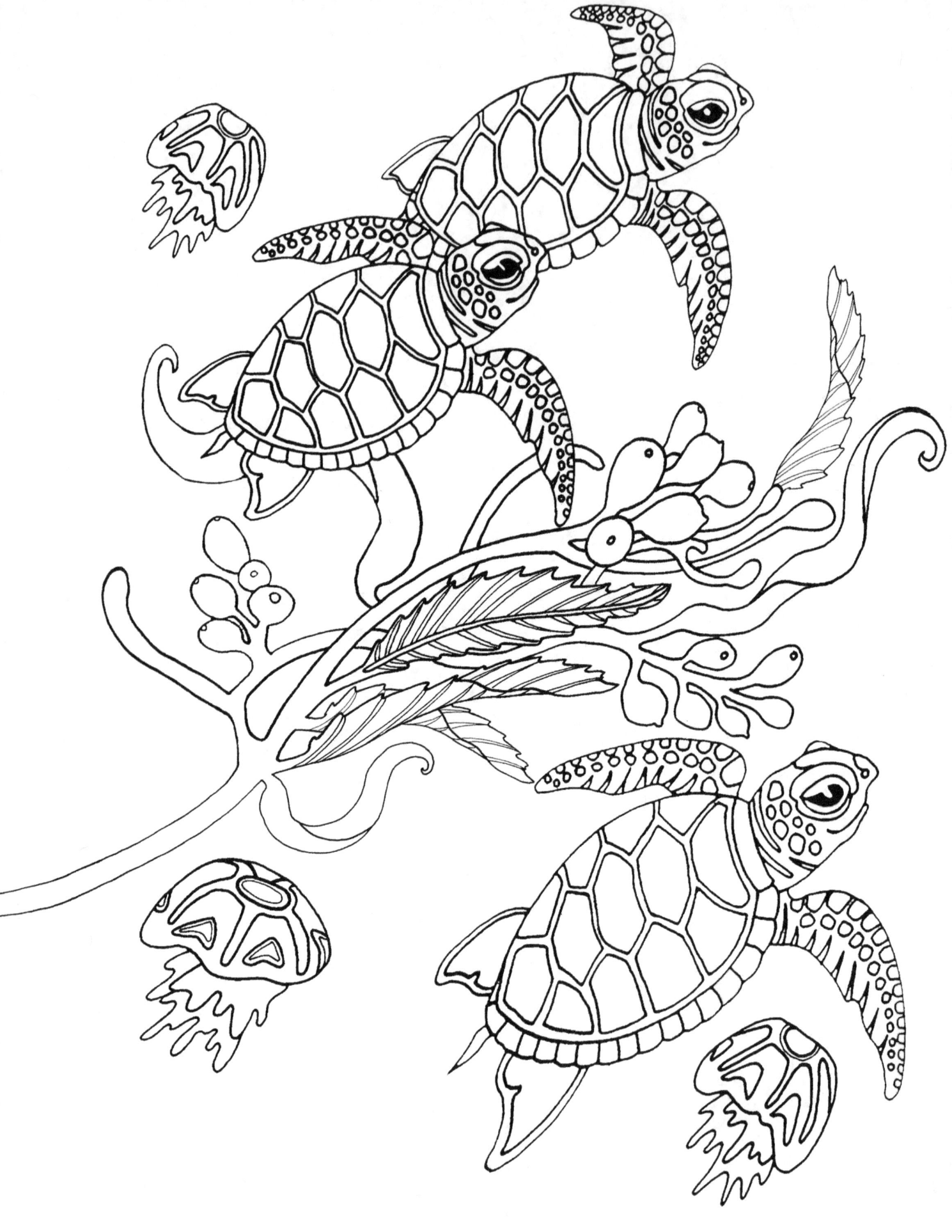

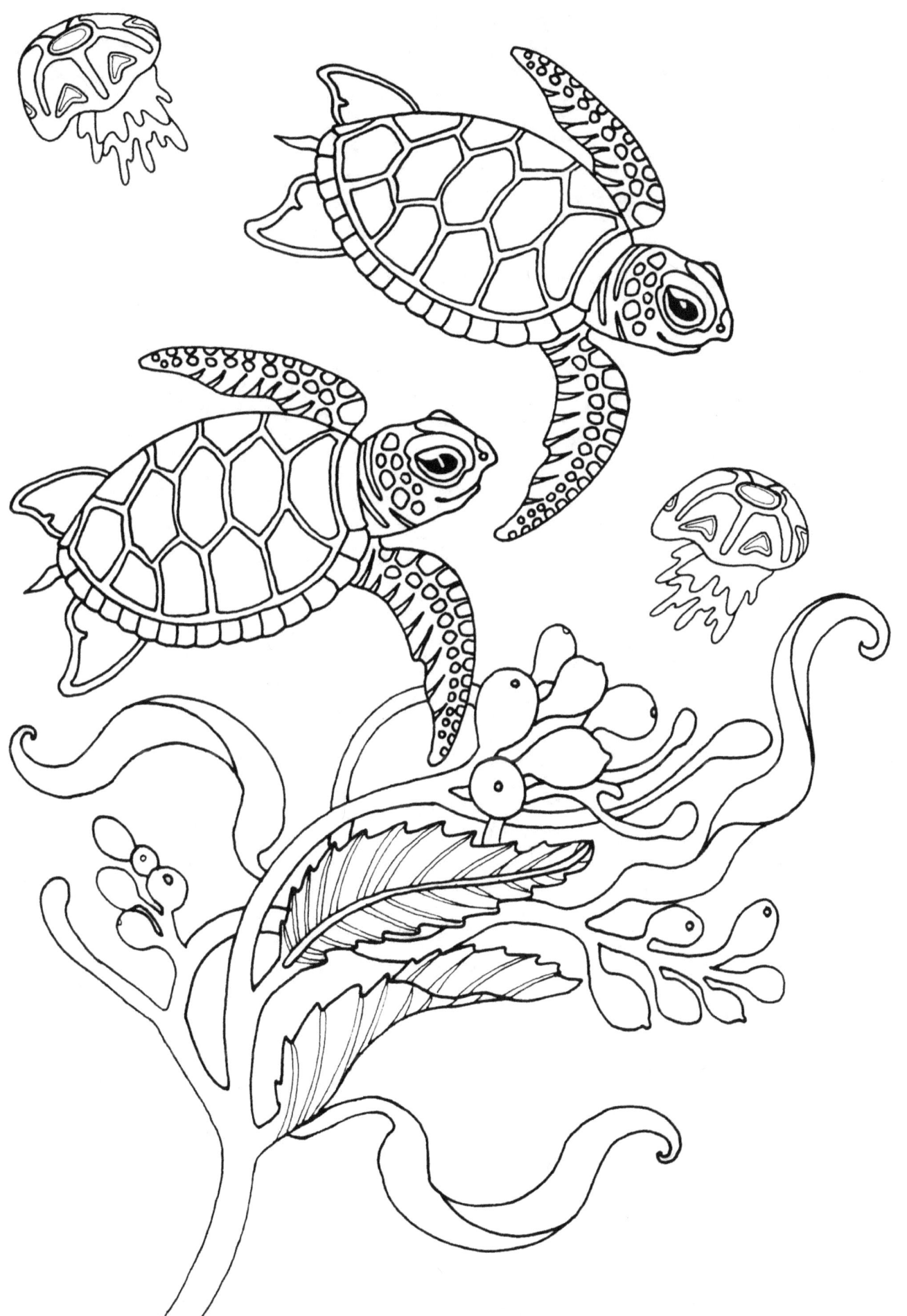

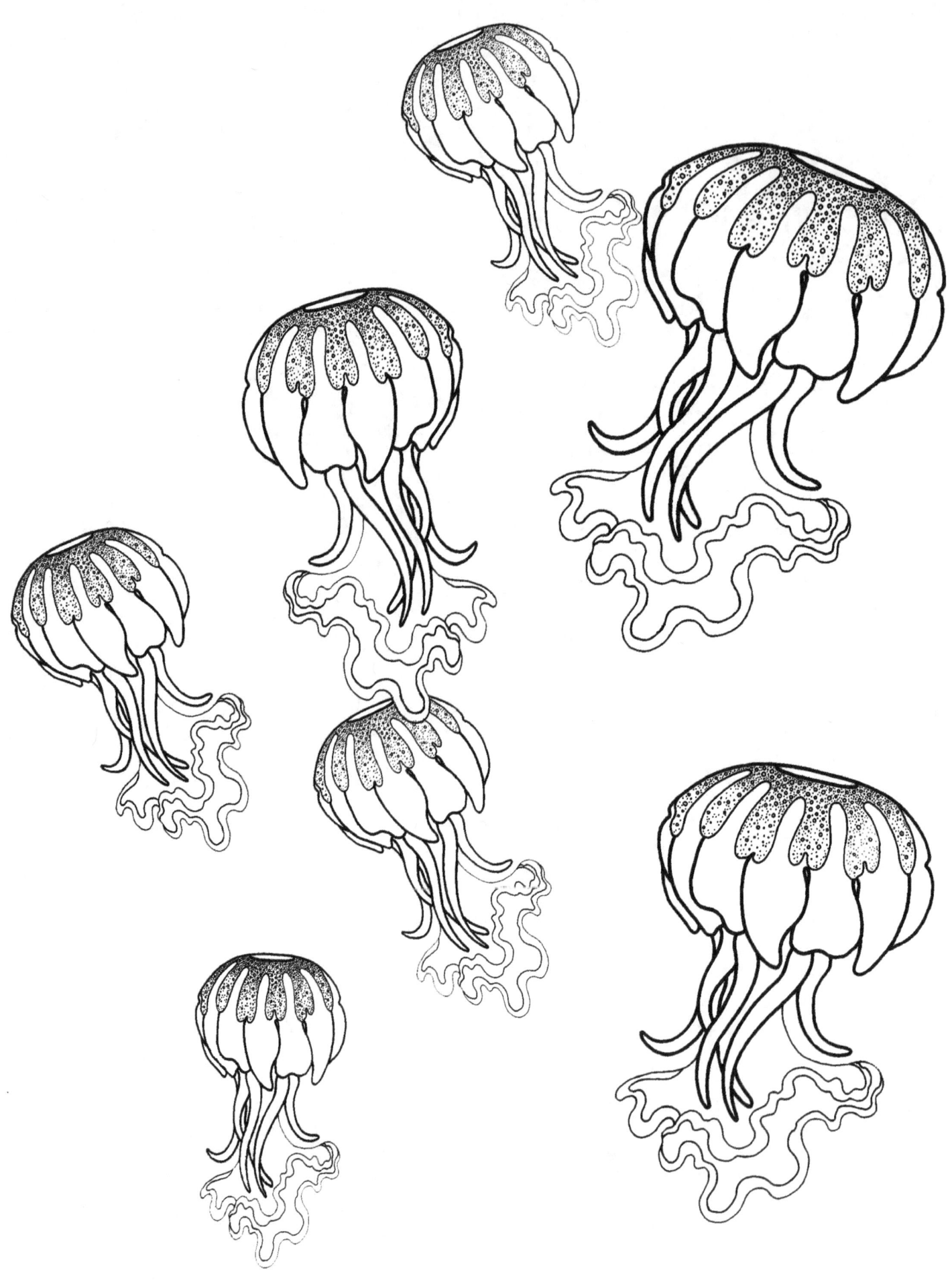

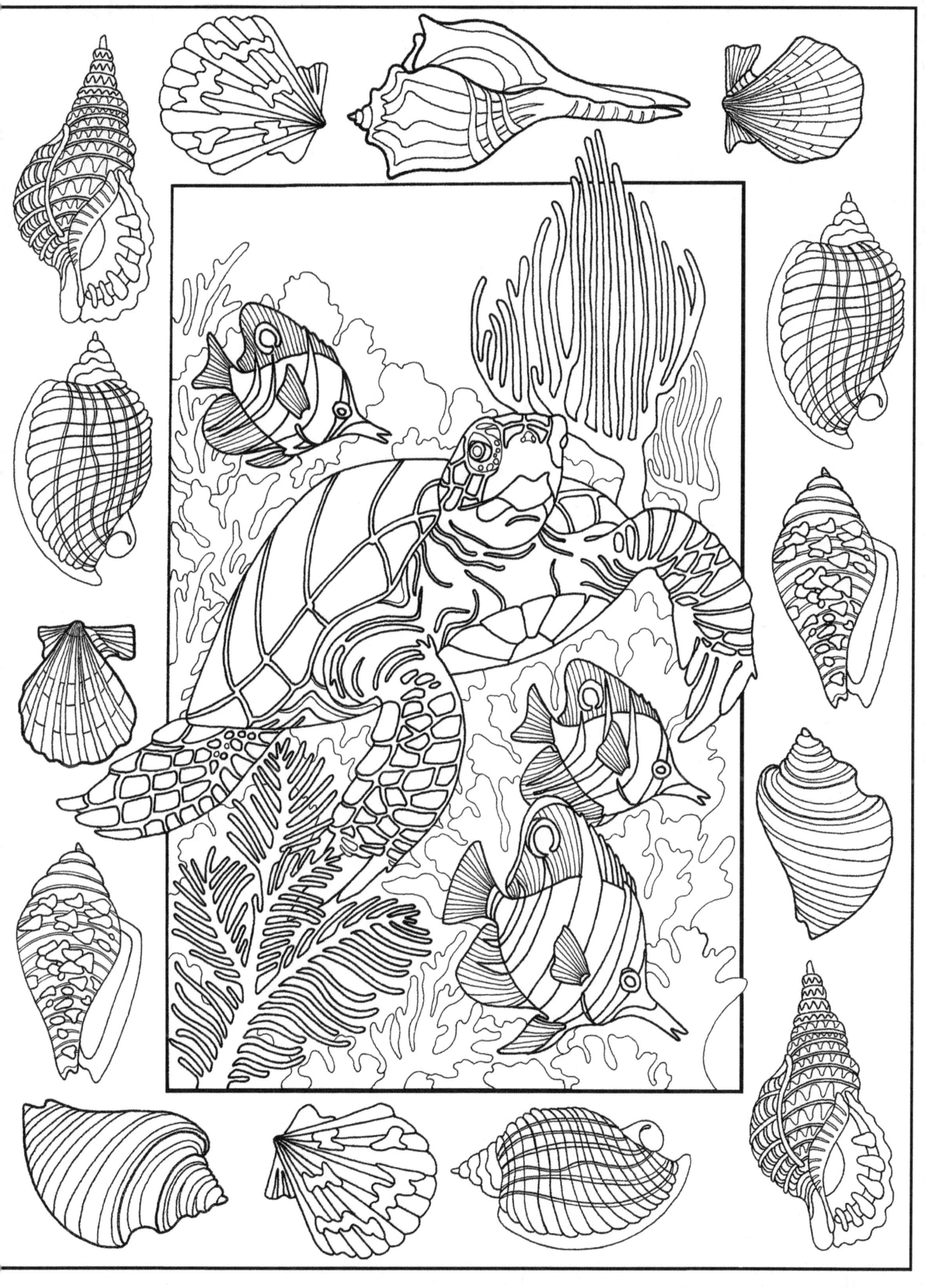

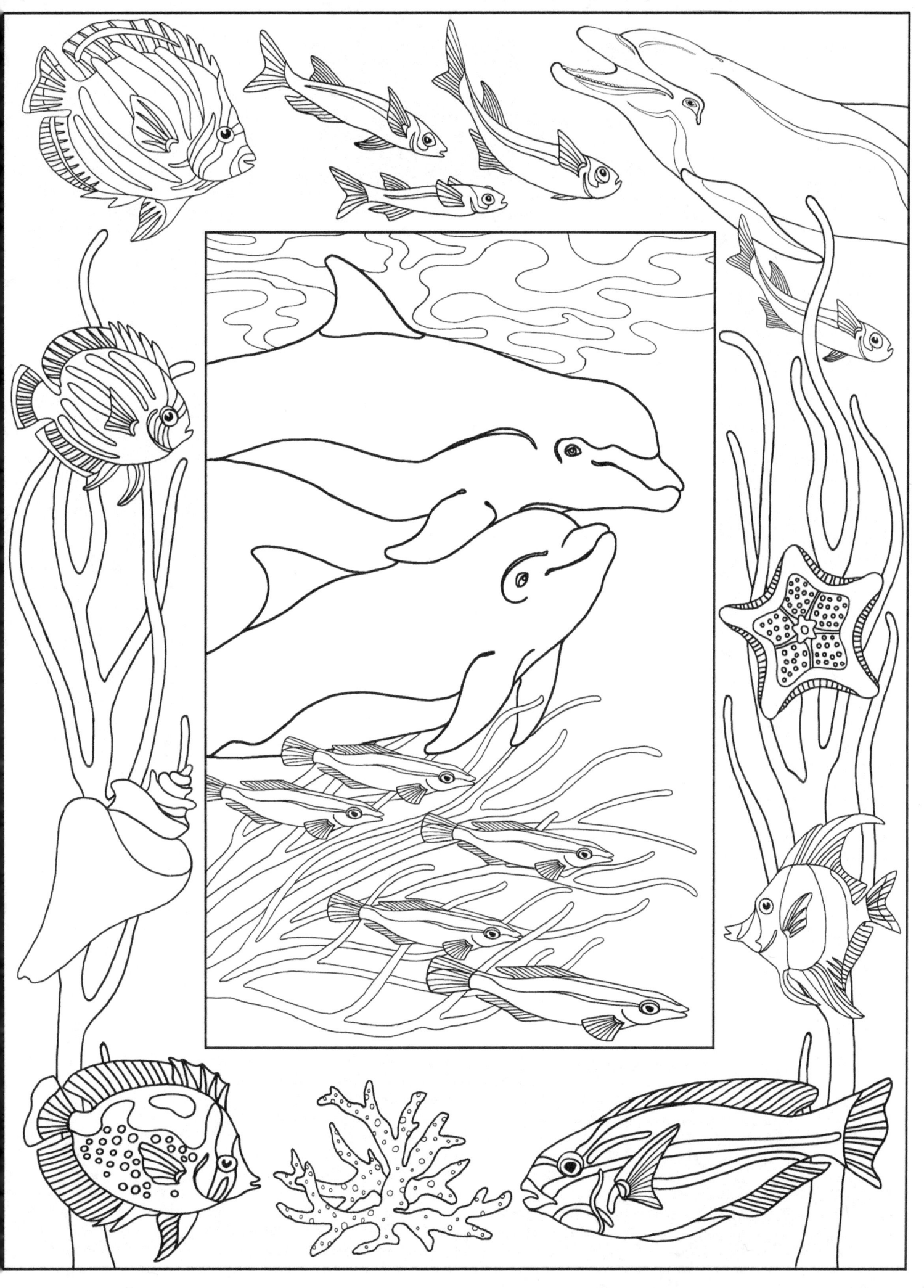